Praise for *Louis Riel and Gabriel Dumont*

"Boyden does a fine job of recounting this fascinating history in a short, readable book.... A thoughtful approach.... Boyden's book serves as a good beginning to reflect on issues and questions that arise from the life of Riel."

—*Brandon Sun*

"Suspenseful and elegantly written."

—*Canada's History* magazine

"As an acclaimed novelist, Boyden intertwines his ability to craft a suspenseful and elegant narrative with the fascinating historical story of Riel and Dumont.... [T]his book is a great read."

—*The Lindsay Post*

"At the heart of Boyden's book is also the fascinating relationship between the intellectual Riel, and the man of action Dumont."

—*The Globe and Mail*

"Boyden's book is short, swif̶t̶ ̶a̶n̶d̶ ̶...
Required reading for Canadia̶...

"[Boyden] brilliantly creates a sense of tension and foreboding from the first page onward."

—*Ottawa Life Magazine*

Praise for the Extraordinary Canadians series

"These books are not definitive biography; rather, they are opportunities to deepen the relationship between Canadians of the past and Canadians of the present. May this dialogue continue, so that today's biographers themselves will be the subject of the next wave of writers."

—*The Globe and Mail*

"The concise books are a vivid, 'character-driven patchwork' of modern Canadian history made relevant to modern readers. In other words, no dry academic tomes allowed.... What's compelling about the Extraordinary Canadians series is that it draws you back to some of the original oeuvres—to Anne, to Carr's remarkable paintings or to Glenn Gould's Goldberg Variations."   —*Vancouver Sun*

"Marvelous."   —*Ottawa Citizen*

"A series to collect and cherish. As ambitious a publishing program as has been seen in years, it is a reminder of how good a biography can be." — *The Sun Times* (Owen Sound)

PENGUIN

LOUIS RIEL & GABRIEL DUMONT

A Canadian of Irish, Scottish, and Métis roots, Joseph Boyden is the award-winning author of *Three Day Road,* which won the Rogers Writers' Trust Fiction Prize and the McNally Robinson Aboriginal Book of the Year Award, and *Through Black Spruce,* which won the Scotiabank Giller Prize. He divides his time between Northern Ontario and Louisiana.

Louis Riel and Gabriel Dumont

by JOSEPH BOYDEN

With an Introduction by
John Ralston Saul
SERIES EDITOR

PENGUIN
an imprint of Penguin Canada

Published by the Penguin Group
Penguin Group (Canada)
90 Eglinton Avenue East, Suite 700, Toronto, Ontario, Canada M4P 2Y3

Penguin Group (USA) Inc., 375 Hudson Street, New York, New York 10014, U.S.A.
Penguin Books Ltd, 80 Strand, London WC2R 0RL, England
Penguin Ireland, 25 St Stephen's Green, Dublin 2, Ireland (a division of Penguin Books Ltd)
Penguin Group (Australia), 707 Collins Street, Melbourne, Victoria 3008, Australia
(a division of Pearson Australia Group Pty Ltd)
Penguin Books India Pvt Ltd, 11 Community Centre, Panchsheel Park,
New Delhi – 110 017, India
Penguin Group (NZ), 67 Apollo Drive, Rosedale, Auckland 0632, New Zealand
(a division of Pearson New Zealand Ltd)
Penguin Books (South Africa) (Pty) Ltd, 24 Sturdee Avenue, Rosebank,
Johannesburg 2196, South Africa

Penguin Books Ltd, Registered Offices: 80 Strand, London WC2R 0RL, England

First published in Penguin hardcover by Penguin Canada, 2010

Published in this edition, 2013

1 2 3 4 5 6 7 8 9 10 (WEB)

Copyright © Joseph Boyden, 2010
Introduction copyright © John Ralston Saul, 2010

Manufactured in Canada.

LIBRARY AND ARCHIVES CANADA CATALOGUING IN PUBLICATION

Boyden, Joseph, 1966–
Louis Riel and Gabriel Dumont / by Joseph Boyden ; with an
introduction by John Ralston Saul.

(Extraordinary Canadians)
Includes bibliographical references.

ISBN 978-0-14-305586-0

1. Riel, Louis, 1844–1885. 2. Dumont, Gabriel, 1837–1906.
3. Métis—Prairie Provinces—Biography. I. Title. II. Series: Extraordinary Canadians

FC3217.1.A1B69 2013   971.05'10922   C2013-900591-9

Visit the Penguin Canada website at **www.penguin.ca**

Special and corporate bulk purchase rates available; please see
www.penguin.ca/corporatesales or call 1-800-810-3104, ext. 2477.

ALWAYS LEARNING   PEARSON

For Gabriel.
For Louis.
And always, for Amanda.

CONTENTS

John Ralston Saul

How do civilizations imagine themselves? One way is for each of us to look at ourselves through our society's most remarkable figures. I'm not talking about hero worship or political iconography. That is a danger to be avoided at all costs. And yet people in every country do keep on going back to the most important people in their past.

This series of Extraordinary Canadians brings together rebels, reformers, martyrs, writers, painters, thinkers, political leaders. Why? What is it that makes them relevant to us so long after their deaths?

For one thing, their contributions are there before us, like the building blocks of our society. More important than that are their convictions and drive, their sense of what is right and wrong, their willingness to risk all, whether it be their lives, their reputations, or simply being wrong in public. Their ideas, their triumphs and failures, all of these somehow constitute a mirror of our society. We look at these people, all dead, and discover what we have been, but also what we can be. A mirror is an instrument for measuring ourselves. What we see can be both a warning and an encouragement.

These eighteen biographies of twenty key Canadians are centred on the meaning of each of their lives. Each of them is very different, but these are not randomly chosen great figures. Together they produce a grand sweep of the creation of modern Canada, from our first steps as a democracy in 1848 to our questioning of modernity late in the twentieth century.

All of them except one were highly visible on the cutting edge of their day while still in their twenties, thirties, and forties. They were young, driven, curious. An astonishing level of fresh energy surrounded them and still does. We in the twenty-first century talk endlessly of youth, but power today is often controlled by people who fear the sort of risks and innovations embraced by everyone in this series. A number of them were dead—hanged, infected on a battlefield, broken by their exertions—well before middle age. Others hung on into old age, often profoundly dissatisfied with themselves.

Each one of these people has changed you. In some cases you know this already. In others you will discover how through these portraits. They changed the way the world hears music, thinks of war, communicates. They changed how each of us sees what surrounds us, how minorities are treated, how we think of immigrants, how we look after each other, how we imagine ourselves through what are now our stories.

You will notice that many of them were people of the word. Not just the writers. Why? Because civilizations are built around many themes, but they require a shared public language. So Laurier, Bethune, Douglas, Riel, LaFontaine, McClung, Trudeau, Lévesque, Big Bear, even Carr and Gould, were masters of the power of language. Beaverbrook was one of the most powerful newspaper publishers of his day. Countries need action and laws and courage. But civilization is not a collection of prime ministers. Words, words, words—it is around these that civilizations create and imagine themselves.

The authors I have chosen for each subject are not the obvious experts. They are imaginative, questioning minds from among our leading writers and activists. They have, each one of them, a powerful connection to their subject. And in their own lives, each is engaged in building what Canada is now becoming.

That is why a documentary is being filmed about each subject. Images are yet another way to get at each subject and to understand their effect on us.

The one continuous, essential voice of biography since 1961 has been the *Dictionary of Canadian Biography*. But there has not been a project of book-length biographies such as Extraordinary Canadians in a hundred years, not since the Makers of Canada series. And yet every generation understands the past differently, and so sees in the mirror of these remarkable figures somewhat different lessons. As history rolls on, some truths remain the same while others are revealed in a new and unexpected way.

What strikes me again and again is just how dramatically ethical decisions figured in these people's lives. They form the backbone of history and memory. Some of them, Big Bear, for example, or Dumont, or even Lucy Maud Montgomery, thought of themselves as failures by the end of their lives. But the ethical cord that was strung taut through their work has now carried them on to a new meaning and even greater strength, long after their deaths.

Each of these stories is a revelation of the tough choices unusual people must make to find their way. And each of us as readers will find in the desperation of the Chinese revolution, the search for truth in fiction, the political and military dramas, different meanings that strike a personal chord. At first it is that personal emotive link to such figures which draws us in. Then we find they are a key that opens the whole society of their time to us. Then we realize that in that 150-year period many of them knew each other, were friends, opposed each other. Finally, when all these stories are put together, you will see that a whole new debate has been created around Canadian civilization and the shape of our continuous experiment.

And in no story does the past reverberate into the present with as much force as that of Louis Riel and Gabriel Dumont. Riel, the great martyr or villain—depending on your point of view—of nineteenth-century Canada, has become the Father of Manitoba, the great Métis leader, and a tragic national hero. Gabriel Dumont, long-time Métis leader, a great buffalo hunter and guerrilla fighter, and one of Canada's most remarkable military leaders, has always been a mysterious figure, somehow cut off from mainstream political reality.

Now the brilliant novelist Joseph Boyden has brought the two men together, back into the relationship that shaped them, shaped modern Métis history, and was central to the shaping of Canada. After all, the tragedy of the Canadian internal war of 1885 showed how badly we could go wrong as a country, how easily and deeply we could scar ourselves, both the victims and the victimizers. But the power of the Riel–Dumont story has turned the tragedy into a lesson.

This balance, this tension of two very different men, shows how their reality and the reality of the Métis people are central to all our lives.

CHAPTER ONE

Awake

Gabriel wakes before the sun. All real hunters do. He tethers his horses to his four-wheel cart. He wishes the squealing axles silent because he knows that they cry out his departure to those who are afraid of him, and to those who wish him great ill. These include the priest, Father André, and that whining dog of a man, the bureaucrat Lawrence Clarke.

Gabriel's wife is used to his early morning departures, has come to expect them and his eventual return, days or weeks or months later, his cart laden with the sustenance of the hunt. But this journey carries great secrecy and great import for the people who have asked him to take it.

Gabriel is not a tall man. He's compact and powerful though, thick as a bull moose through the chest, with the black eyes of a crow, the beard of the French, and the high cheekbones of the Sarcee. He is the leader of the buffalo hunt, a position of high respect and huge skill as well as crushing demand. The buffalo are mostly gone now, and the Métis people fall back on what they've always fallen back on in tight times: their farms here, in what is now Saskatchewan, laid out Red River style, long and narrow, using the riverfront for their thirst. Métis and crops alike need water, first and foremost. And the Métis allotments are sensible for this landscape.

But Gabriel is not a farmer. He knows that anyone who wishes to head west, or east for that matter, has to cross the wide and pretty South Saskatchewan River. With no buffalo to pursue, he's built himself a good business here where the Carlton Trail nears Batoche. He runs a river ferry, and because Gabriel is a social man, he's constructed a small store as an excuse for visitors to come in. When they do, they're always surprised to find a billiards table at the centre of the room. There's nothing Gabriel enjoys more than a good game, and he's a talented player, rarely losing. Gabriel's known across the North-West not only for his skills as a hunter and a leader but for his social skills, too. He's a well-respected man.

Canada has just turned seventeen, is prone to the moods and fears and stubbornness of a teenager. Surveyors, at the behest of John A. Macdonald, have arrived to tell the Métis that the Métis' understanding of their environment does not correspond with Ottawa's. The surveyors are just working men, for the most part, and must take little joy in squaring off imaginary parcels of wilderness. But their work inflames the Métis. The Métis, after all, have been pushed farther and farther west, following the buffalo, following a life in the wilds. They are a people of the land. The freedom and difficulty of the land is what they know.

And now that the American Civil War is a staunched but still festering wound, that hungry nation to the south looks north and west toward Manifest Destiny to try to quell its other appetites. The government of Canada understands this acutely, pushing its surveyors westward as fast as the surveyors can plot out squares of earth. A Canadian railroad, a sea-to-sea iron horse, is the only way to show the Americans that Canada is not a part of their destiny. Métis be damned if they will slow this progress.

To the men in Ottawa, the mixed-bloods are insolent and stubborn. The Métis represent two painful thorns in John A. Macdonald's feet as he attempts his Anglo-Saxon stride to the Pacific. One foot swells with the Indian problem, the other with the French. While often illiterate, the Métis are better organized politically than the Indians. And they have a wanderlust that the Québécois do not. The Métis are both Indian and French. And they are neither. To make matters worse for Sir John, the Métis' growing understanding that their actions have consequences Ottawa cannot ignore stems from the grassroots actions of one man, a man Sir John has long wished dead or gone. His name is Louis Riel.

Yes, the Métis are complicated in that they are half-bloods. The European blood—more often French, but also Scots, Irish, or English—understands but still despises the work of the surveyor. The Indian blood—Cree, Ojibwa and Saulteaux, Sarcee, Peguis, Blood, Blackfoot, Gros Ventre, Dene, among others—this Indian blood struggles against ownership of land by humans, and especially governments. But the Métis learned a hard lesson in Manitoba a number of years ago—that if they do not have title to their land, the bureaucrats in Ottawa sell it to others, to newcomers or men representing vested interests. And so far, the government has turned a deaf ear to Métis petitions for fair title to the land that they now settle and live on.

Gabriel, who sets out on his secret journey south early that June morning, is a man who's always been ruled more by his Indian blood. He has lived off and from the land his whole life. He is a Métis leader whom the Indians see as a chief, respected and feared by those who've met him. As a young man, barely a teenager, he was forced to kill Sioux attackers at Grand Coteau. He can shoot a duck's head clean off at a hundred paces, is one of the few who can call buffalo by mimicking the grunt of the bull, the whine of the cow.

Gabriel is a master horseman, and besides French and a smattering of English, he speaks six Indian languages despite the fact that he cannot read or write.

Intelligence and wisdom, though, cannot be quantified by these abilities, especially in the wild lands of the Canadian West in 1884. After all, it would be a great joke to try to imagine a politician from Upper Canada surviving more than a couple of days in this beautiful but harsh place that the Métis have settled as they push farther and farther away from Ottawa, as they search for their own belonging, Israelites in a very different setting, in a very different time.

And so Gabriel, captain of the hunt, a role passed down from his father and his father's father, leaves his home before sunrise so as not to inform those who wish him ill and begins the ride south, seven hundred miles through rolling prairie, with three trusted allies—one French Métis, one an English half-breed, the third his brother-in-law. Two others join them for a while but decide not to complete the journey.

What Gabriel doesn't know, though, is that the local factor of the Hudson's Bay Company, that dog Lawrence Clarke, has heard the whisperings of Gabriel's secret mission and has sent an urgent wire to government officials saying action must be taken and Gabriel stopped. Clarke's an excitable man and has had run-ins with Gabriel in the past, has even tried to have him arrested. Clarke claims that Gabriel wishes to start a rebellion and is not afraid of bloodshed. Clarke says many demeaning things about the Métis, but what Clarke doesn't say is that he himself is set to profit financially and politically if Gabriel Dumont and his ilk fail in their mission. What's so sadly ironic is that bloodshed is indeed on the horizon, plenty of it, and much of the blame can be placed squarely on the shoulders of Lawrence Clarke.

WHILE DUMONT KNOWS his own country as only the leader of the buffalo hunt can, his seven-hundred-mile trip south from Batoche into Montana is one he's never travelled before. It fills him with the excitement of adult purpose but also the wanderlust of his youth. He's not seen this new land south of what is today the city of Saskatoon, country as pretty as his own, the prairie awakening in late May with rosy everlasting, purple rock cress, shining arnica and ground plum, larkspur, shooting star, and prairie onion.

Those who have never seen prairies imagine them as nothing more than mile after mile of flat and redundant land. This is far from the truth. The earth unfolds in slow rises and low dips under Gabriel's cart wheels, and he keeps a sharp eye for possible enemies who might be hiding in the bunches of cottonwood, burr oak, or trembling aspen or in the deeper valleys leading to rivers. He easily avoids the North West Mounted Police patrols. They are noisy and leave their mark wherever they go. It's the hostile bands of Indians who might see him as an unwanted visitor that worry him most. But as it turns out, the Blackfoot of this part of Canada know him and welcome him; they suggest routes he might take to slip into the United States.

Averaging forty miles a day, Dumont and his party wind through the Cypress Hills, the haunt and hiding place of whisky runners and smugglers. Eventually he crosses into the States near Fort Assiniboine, Montana. The party knows to follow the Missouri River to where it meets another river called the Sun. Now Gabriel must worry about avoiding the U.S. Army patrols and Indians who don't know his reputation. Indeed, the story goes that Gabriel and his group come across a group of Gros Ventres who've not traded with the Métis before. But in Gabriel's forthright and charismatic way, he talks his way out of paying for passage through the tribe's land.

Early on the seventeenth morning, on June 4, with spring now in full bloom, Gabriel and his emissaries ride into Saint Peter's Mission, a small and poverty-racked community of mostly Blackfeet. Finding the man they've come for proves easy in such a little place. An old woman informs the travellers that Louis Riel is attending mass, his daily custom. Dumont asks her to go into the church and tell Riel of the visitors who need to speak to him urgently. If Dumont is nervous about meeting this man upon whom the Métis of Canada have decided to pin their hopes, he knows not to show it.

Looking back into history, into the past, invariably leads to disagreement. Some say that Dumont and Riel had already come across each other during the Métis struggles in Manitoba in 1870, fourteen years before. Others say that Dumont and Riel had never met in person but had only corresponded through one or two letters of support Dumont had asked others to write on his behalf and then sent to Riel those many years ago.

What does appear clear from the works of prominent Canadian historians like George Woodcock and Maggie Siggins is that when Riel, a black-bearded man with the intense eyes of a prophet, emerged from the church, he did not recognize Dumont. And according to Woodcock, Dumont's pre-eminent biographer, Riel approached and took Dumont's hand in his own, saying, "You seem to be a man from far away. I do not know you, but you seem to know me."

If these words hurt Dumont, again he does not show it. Instead, Gabriel replies, "Indeed I do, and I think you should know me as well. Don't you know the name of Gabriel Dumont?"

It is only now that Riel's eyes spark with recognition. Every Métis knows the name of one of their great hunters and chiefs. After a couple more pleasantries, Riel informs the men he needs to return to mass, pointing out the way to his cabin where his wife, Marguerite, will offer them something to eat.

Later that day, Riel listens as Dumont and his companions explain the concerns of the Métis back in Canada. The federal government has been sending surveyors, and as they all know so well, when surveyors appear they are hated and feared more than locusts on the horizon because outsiders hungry for land soon follow. Although the Métis have settled in the areas around places like Batoche and Saint-Laurent for many years, even generations, the government refuses to recognize the Métis' stake in their own land, is in fact telling the Métis that their way of allotting land in the Red River style won't be recognized. In the eyes of John A. Macdonald, the Métis are nothing more than squatters.

The buffalo are all but gone, and the Métis desperately need the basic insurance of their small plots for subsistence farming. But the prime minister refuses to even admit he's received their many petitions. Clearly, the government has no qualms about ignoring the Métis and their land, culture, and rights. The government hopes that if it ignores the Métis problem long enough, the problem will cease to exist.

Dumont, despite his illiteracy, is a wise man. He knows that Riel will recognize how history seems to repeat itself. Doesn't all of this sound so similar to what happened in Manitoba fourteen years before? The Métis' rights are trampled, the authorities expect them to behave sheepishly and accept their lot (or lack thereof), and the work of nation-building can resume, government and big business—in the form of the Hudson's Bay Company—marching ever westward, hand-in-hand.

But a decade and a half ago, grounded by his deep faith in Catholicism and backed by the determination of his people not to be trodden upon, Louis Riel made a stand for the Métis. The government eventually, stubbornly, recognized that if Manitoba were to be admitted as a province of the confederation, it would be wise to accept the Métis' petitions and grant them some parcels of land. To try to quash this belligerent group of half-breeds, inflaming along the way relations with the Indians and the Québécois alike, didn't make the sense that acquiescence did.

The price of resistance proved high for Riel, though. Despite eventually being voted into Parliament as a member, he was so hated by the English Protestants that a bounty was put upon his head by no less a figure than the premier of Ontario. A quiet and sour deal with John A. Macdonald banishing Riel from Canada followed. And like an Israelite prophet, Riel has wandered the northern border of the United States from Vermont to Minnesota to Montana ever since, dreaming of his return to his own promised land.

This repetition of events separated by fifteen years, this back-and-forth between the Métis and the Canadians, maybe it's all really a game, like billiards. Shoot straight and leave your opponent with only the options you wish him to have. Force him to scratch then take advantage. But John A. Macdonald refuses to even come to the table, refuses to even admit that Gabriel, the Métis, own their own table. Gabriel understands that when the government hears that Louis Riel has returned from his banishment, it will have to come, will have to play this game of strategy with the half-breeds.

And, smart billiards player that Dumont is, he lays out the table for Riel, then petitions him to come and once again play the game Riel cannot resist. Dumont assumes that Riel hasn't lost his fire, that his love for his people will dictate that he come back home with Dumont and company to try to leverage the Canadians in the proper way.

Riel's well-documented answer to the mission's plea is classic Riel in that to the outsider it sounds bizarre, even a bit mad. But to those who know Riel well, especially in these last years wandering the wilds of America, maybe it makes its own strange sense.

"God wants you to understand," Riel begins, the four men listening intently at his table, "that you have taken the right way, for there are four of you, and you have arrived on the fourth of June. And you wish to have a fifth to return with you. I cannot give you my answer today. Wait until tomorrow morning, and I will have a decision for you."

Does Riel's coyly bizarre response concern Gabriel? If so, he never speaks of it, though Gabriel confesses that he never forgets Riel's words. At this point, maybe he and company view Riel as a mystic, a man in tune with energies not understood or felt by the commoner. Or maybe some niggling doubt worms its way into the base of Gabriel's spine, forcing him to question the wisdom of travelling this far to ask a man who might not be totally sane to lead the people to freedom.

Many possibilities must go through Dumont's mind the rest of that day and that evening as he awaits Riel's answer. Wouldn't it be easy to view Joan of Arc as insane? Or any of the Biblical prophets? What about Jesus himself? Not that Gabriel would ever compare Riel to Jesus, for that would be blasphemy. No one can disagree that something hot burns inside Riel, so hot that his eyes themselves, when he speaks passionately, seem to be on fire. And wasn't it Riel who brought the Métis some justice so many years ago? He is one of the first Métis to be university educated. He is a man of God, and a person who has walked in the great halls of the white man's power. What other choice do the Métis of Saskatchewan have, this disparate group whose every petition the government ignores? Riel knows the government's game, and he has proven that he gets results. Dumont and the others can put up with his oddities and rather extreme religious views. It's a small price to pay for the recognition of their rights. Right? How well must Dumont sleep the night of June 4, 1884, awaiting an answer from this Métis prophet in whose home he rests his head?

At Riel's request, Dumont joins him at mass early the next morning. Dumont is not especially religious, not by a long stretch, but he respects the Church and understands its great power in the lives of the deeply religious Métis. Dumont needs the blessing of priests like Father André and Bishop Grandin back home if he is to move forward with the plan of creating a permanent homeland for his people, either within the confederacy of Canada or separate from it. But as of late, Father André, the priest for the parish of Batoche, has been straining against any talk of pursuing rights through anything beyond letter writing. Today, if Riel agrees to come home to Canada, his deep spirituality, Dumont knows, will be as good as any priest's blessing in calming Métis fears that they might be, in any way, acting against God.

Riel, playing the moment as well as any actor in a stage play, allows tension to build all day before he gives his answer. He finally agrees to come back to Canada with Dumont and company, but only if his wife and two young children can join him. Dumont readily agrees. There's plenty of room for all in the wagons. Riel explains that he must finish up his teaching at the mission school as he'd made a promise to the children, but this will take only three or four days. Again, Dumont says that this will not pose a problem.

"Fifteen years ago," Riel says, "I gave my heart to my nation, and I am ready to give it again." He then sits down and writes a long letter to the men in the room while they stand about awkwardly. When he is finished, Riel hands the letter to Michel Dumas, who is able to read.

Riel, in part, writes:

> Your invitation is cordial and pressing. You ask me
> to accompany you with my family. I could make

my excuses and say no. Yet you await my decision, so that all I have to do is to make my own preparations, and the letters you bring assure me that I would be welcomed by those who have sent you as if I were returning to my own family. Gentlemen, your visit honours and pleases me, and your role as delegates gives it the character of a memorable event; I record it as one of the happiest occasions of my life. It is an event my family will remember, and I pray to God that your deputation may be one of the blessings of this year, which is the fortieth of my existence.

Let me speak briefly and frankly. I doubt if any advice I could give you while on this alien soil concerning matters in Canada would be of much use beyond the frontier. But there is another aspect of the matter. According to Article 31 of the Manitoba treaty, the Canadian government owes me two hundred and forty acres of land. It also owes me five lots which are valuable because of their hay, their wood, and their nearness to the river. These lots belonged to me according to various paragraphs of the same Article 31 of the treaty to which I have referred. Directly or indirectly, the

Canadian government has deprived me of these properties. In addition, if the Canadian government were to examine the matter, it would soon see that it owes me something more than that.

These claims which I have on the government retain their validity in spite of the fact that I have now become an American citizen. In your interest therefore and in mine as well, I accept your friendly invitation; I will go and spend a little time among you. Perhaps by presenting petitions to the government we shall be able to gain at least something. But my intention is to come back here soon, in the coming autumn.

Most every scholar of Riel has remarked upon the strange internal dichotomy that induced him to at once aggrandize and doubt himself. They also make note of this letter, among many others, for various reasons, often to help support wide-ranging hypotheses about Riel and his intentions. Some argue that his intentions in 1884 are anything but religious. Instead, Riel sees Dumont's invitation as a chance to claim what he believes the government owes him. Others argue that Riel has no idea of the hornet's nest he's about to stir up, that he expects to visit for only a few months to help create petitions before returning to his exile. Still others argue that the letter reflects the scattered and self-important thoughts of a mentally ill man.

But the men to whom the letter is written see it as something else entirely. As his biographer George Woodcock notes, Gabriel is truly humbled by the ascetic conditions in which they find the great Riel and his family living. The Father of Manitoba, a man who should be housed as comfortably as any politician in his mansion in Ottawa, ekes out an existence teaching poor Indian children to read and write. Riel lives in the spirit of Christ himself, having given up all his worldly possessions for the sake of others. This, in the end, comforts Dumont, reassures him that he has indeed done the right thing in travelling this far to petition this great man who can deliver the Métis justice.

On June 10, 1884, Gabriel and company with Louis and family begin the long wagon ride back to Batoche. The warmth and promise of the approaching summer shines down, and their trip home can be viewed as far more than just a literal one. Through great beauty but also great danger, the Métis travel the path they'd taken not long before, a journey that all of them believe leads them back to their homeland.

CHAPTER TWO

Transformation

In many ways, Louis Riel is a man without a home. Born in Red River near Winnipeg in current-day Manitoba in 1844, Louis is the eldest of eleven children. Red River remains his spiritual home in so many ways, but at the tender age of fourteen, his deeply spiritual convictions are recognized by the powerful Bishop Taché, who talks Louis's parents into allowing their son to pursue a university education and the priesthood in Montreal. Louis's relationship with his family, especially his father, is very close, and the decision to let him move so far away is painful for all of them, though his parents must take a certain amount of pride in knowing that their son will become one of the first Métis to be university educated.

Louis is recognized as a very good student, though one prone to dark moodiness, and his years at the Collège de Montréal pass by accordingly. But in 1864, word of his father's sudden death reaches Louis. This shakes him to his core, and by the following spring Louis has withdrawn from the college and been kicked out of the convent of the Grey Nuns, where he attempted to be a day student. He no longer speaks of becoming a priest. He remains in Montreal, taking on a job as a law clerk, a rather dull profession to which he is ill suited. Over the course of this year, Riel falls for a young woman and wishes to marry her but her parents refuse him, in no small part because he is Métis. Riel's friends claim that his broken heart takes him to Chicago, where he stays with the poet Louis-Honoré Fréchette and continues to write his own poetry, a passion of his for many years. From Chicago, Riel makes his way to Saint Paul, Minnesota, where he takes on another clerking job.

In 1868, four years after his father's death, word trickles down of Métis troubles back in Red River. Riel's mother asks him to return home, and Louis, unhappy with the course his life is taking, agrees to return. His first wandering in the wilderness comes to an end on July 26, 1868.

Back home, Riel finds that an influx of English-speaking Protestant settlers have arrived in Red River, and tensions between these new arrivals, the Indians, and the Métis are on the rise. Despite their long tenure on the land around Red River, the Métis don't hold clear title to it according to the Hudson's Bay Company. The Company claims that it actually owns a huge swath of the North-West, a place they call

Rupert's Land, including all of what is now Manitoba. It was given to the Company in 1670 by the King of England, of all people. Now the Company has made a deal to sell Rupert's Land to Canada, and neither seems to care very much what the Métis might feel. The Métis, not considered white, not considered Indian, these people who speak French, English, and a dozen First Nations tongues, as well as their own hybrid one, Michif, are beginning to feel as if they exist in some netherworld that renders them invisible to the rest of the world.

Back home in the bosom of his tight-knit family, Louis feels more grounded than he has in years. He watches what's happening around him with the intense eyes of an osprey, sees how more new Orange settlers from Ontario arrive every month, how the Hudson's Bay Company manoeuvres in its approaching deal with the Canadians, keeping vital information about the sale of land that many feel isn't even the company's a secret from the Métis and Indians.

The Red River Settlement in 1869 has become a vibrant place, an open door to the west, a community of close to twelve thousand and growing. Of those twelve thousand, six thousand are French-speaking Métis, four thousand are English-speaking Métis, and the other approximately two thousand are European and Canadian settlers. Louis

JOSEPH BOYDEN

witnesses how both the government of Canada and the Hudson's Bay Company ignore Métis petitions to be involved in any transactions regarding the land upon which they live. And he especially takes note of the arrival of Canadian surveyors on August 20, 1869. They begin to measure and divide parcels of land in the English-style square lots, ignoring the fact that the Métis, long inhabitants of this place, divide the land in the seigneurial way, each lot narrow and having access to the river. Just as importantly, the Métis have created community lots for livestock grazing, a cornerstone of their society that is deeply rooted in their First Nations beliefs of sharing. All of this is what makes sense in this part of the country. It's clear to anyone who wishes to read between the lines that the Métis will be evicted and thrown to the winds once this deal between the Company and Canada is made.

Feeling the fire of God speak to him once again, a gorgeous deep burn in the pit of his belly that Louis hasn't felt in years, he gives a speech in late August to French and English half-breeds alike from the steps of the deeply symbolic Saint-Boniface Cathedral, denouncing the unfairness of the surveys and the machinations of the Hudson's Bay Company and the government. That many people not only gather but listen and are moved by Louis's powerful words doesn't surprise his family. Louis's departed father, after all, had been instrumental years before in breaking up a Hudson's Bay Company monopoly and remains highly respected for it, even in death. Maybe Louis feels his father's smile that late August day. The crowd is impressed, delighted that they have such an eloquent spokesman who seems a natural to lead them in their struggles. This Louis Riel has spent years out east learning the ways of the Canadians, he is deeply spiritual, and he comes from excellent stock. Louis's position as a leader is quickly cemented, and he finally feels as if he is coming into his own. He understands at last that God doesn't wish him to be a priest. God tells Louis that his role is to stand up for his people, to be their spokesman.

This is a job he takes to quickly. But on that late August day, no one in the crowd guesses that within months Louis will lead them in what the Canadians call a full-scale rebellion—despite the fact that the area isn't even a part of Canada yet—and the Métis call a resistance, a defence of their homeland.

On October 11, 1869, a group of Métis that includes Riel take their first physical action in a course of events that plays out quickly. The English surveyors who'd first appeared near Red River in late August, just nine days after Louis's first speech, continue to busily mark out square parcels of land right on the half-breeds' doorstep. Louis and company confront the survey team on this crisp autumn day, stepping on their chain as a symbolic act of defiance, at the same time putting the fear of God into them.

Louis knows he has no other choice. The Canadians and the Hudson's Bay Company have agreed that December 1, just fifty short days away, is the day this questionable transaction will close. The Métis have tried all other courses. The Roman Catholic Bishop Taché of Red River, the Anglican bishop of Rupert's Land Robert Machray, and even the Hudson's Bay Company governor of Rupert's Land and Assiniboia William Mactavish have all warned the young government of Prime Minister John A. Macdonald that surveying this land in front of the Métis without recognizing Métis title will cause serious unrest. But John A. ignores these important men and the Métis in general, a troubling habit that becomes ingrained over the next many years.

To be fair, John A. is under tremendous pressure to try to carve a western part of this brand new country out of the wilderness before the growing American talk of annexation becomes reality. He feels as if he's in a race with a huge and powerful competitor who disdains, even ridicules him. But John A. Macdonald's often-rash decisions and his callous refusal to recognize the Métis petitions can be viewed as his own racist disdain for these people. It must be God's great joke to create a race that is composed of three such deeply troubled identities: French, Indian, and Catholic, all rolled into one! This people called the Métis, what a nightmare. Thankfully, they are mostly ignorant buffalo hunters and their population is small enough that they don't deserve too much attention. That John A. dares to rub salt into the wounds of this people by appointing the notoriously anti-French William McDougall as lieutenant governor of the North-West Territories in September of 1869 and isn't able to see the quick fallout of this provocation, which culminates just a few weeks later in Riel and company halting the surveyors, spells brewing trouble. It boils over before the Canadian government knows what's happening.

In part, John A. doesn't want to recognize that this Louis Riel is adept at inclusion and has convinced many English half-breeds, European settlers, and a number of Indian tribes that they must stand up in unity if they are to hold any sway on their own land. Louis understands that this newly minted country of Canada is just two years old, and it acts like a bully who's going to have trouble backing up its aggressive tactics. And Louis knows that this resistance doesn't just end with stepping on a chain.

To organize themselves better, the Métis create what they call the "Métis National Committee," and it is in place just five days after the disruption of the surveyors. Louis agrees to become secretary and continues his policy of inclusion, inviting two representatives from each parish to help the Métis and other Red River settlers create an organized stand. The Hudson's Bay Company, fearing its very fruitful deal with Canada might be in jeopardy, becomes involved, asking to meet with the committee to explain itself. It mustn't come as a surprise to the Hudson's Bay Company's Assiniboia Council that the Métis oppose the placement of the anti-French McDougall to the powerful position of lieutenant governor of the whole area, and they warn the council that he will not be welcome to take up his position on their land. McDougall represents all the dangers the Métis face, and all their fears. He represents an encroaching government, the Métis believe, that frowns upon their hunting and subsistence-farming lifestyle, their religious beliefs, and their language. None of the Métis ways will be protected if the Canadians take control of Red River as planned. Simply put, McDougall will be turned back if he attempts to come here without the Canadians first negotiating a fair deal that includes protection of the Métis lifestyle and of the population in general.

The Hudson's Bay Company can't directly control John A.'s political choices, they claim, and William McDougall and entourage arrive in the area in early November. Louis recognizes that the Hudson's Bay Company and the Canadian government work in such unison that it will take a strike against both of them for the two powerhouse entities to listen. As promised, the Métis show up in force on November 2, 1869, and physically prevent McDougall from coming any farther, actually scaring him enough that he retreats to North Dakota. It is about this time that the Métis, their sense of humour intact, give McDougall the nickname Wandering Willie.

Louis's call for the Métis to stand up for themselves has worked in the last brief months, and the number of resisters has swelled. This day that Riel turns away McDougall becomes truly monumental when Riel makes the boldest move of his life. With four hundred followers behind him, he strikes at the Hudson's Bay Company's physical symbol of authority in this country, Fort Garry, and takes it over in a bloodless coup. There's no turning back now.

Both John A. and the Hudson's Bay Company are forced to recognize that the Red River Métis are suddenly a force to be reckoned with. Maybe it's just luck, but the Métis' timing is impeccable. The Canadian government isn't to take over control of this area for close to another month, and the Hudson's Bay Company doesn't have a standing army that can dislodge the Métis. Besides, for either the government or the Company to attempt to react with physical force is far too politically dangerous, time-consuming, and expensive a proposal.

Now that Riel and the Métis find themselves in a rare position of power, they know that in order to succeed they need to centre it on a governing body that's not just representative of the Métis but of all settlers. By late November they propose a provisional government consisting equally of English settlers and Métis that will negotiate directly with the Canadian government. But not all of the English are happy. Some are upset with how Riel has treated McDougall by turning him away, others don't believe that Métis and English views dovetail, and others are simply so racist that the idea of existing on an equal basis with people who are not only French and Indian but Catholic is a ludicrous notion.

A number of this minority, all of them English, led by Dr. John Christian Schultz and Charles Mair, call themselves the Canadian Party and try to rally others living in and around Red River, but most ignore their call. Dr. Schultz manages to raise about four dozen recruits, whom he uses to guard his house and store. He's a well-to-do merchant in town, after all, and he's been one of the most vocal opponents of Riel and the Métis.

Riel understands that he cannot allow such a threat to continue and orders Schultz's house surrounded. Schultz and company surrender on December 7 and are imprisoned in Fort Garry. Included in the group is a particularly belligerent and angry Orangeman named Thomas Scott who takes great pleasure, it seems, in tormenting his captors.

On December 8, riding the groundswell of success and support, Riel achieves his goal of forming a provisional government. The council demands that it should represent Métis and settler grievances, but Riel has no reason to believe that this council is best for the Métis, and it is agreed that his new government will enter direct negotiations with Canada.

Just over a week before, on December 1, McDougall had foolishly declared himself the lieutenant governor of the North-West in absentia, not knowing that the Canadians had postponed the idea of taking over Rupert's Land from the Hudson's Bay Company when news of Métis unrest had reached Ottawa. McDougall, looking the fool, retreats to Ontario, and the vacuum of power is quickly filled by Riel and the provisional government. The Hudson's Bay Company, John A. Macdonald, and the English Protestants who oppose the Métis are all left reeling, asking themselves how this could have happened. John A. must realize that he will now be forced to enter into discussion with the Métis, and hopefully cut any early losses.

Over the course of the rest of December and well into January, the situation between Red River and Ottawa remains tense. John A. allows Governor General Lord Lisgar to declare an amnesty for any Red River Métis who will lay down their arms, but this goes basically ignored. John A. then sends the French Canadians Abbé Jean-Baptiste Thibault and Charles-René d'Irumberry de Salaberry to speak with the Métis, but the two men have little power to negotiate anything of importance. Eventually Hudson's Bay representative Donald Alexander Smith is appointed by Ottawa with more authority to negotiate.

Riel is elected president of the provisional government shortly after Christmas, and on January 19 and 20 he makes headway in negotiations when Smith promises Red River inhabitants, who are all now firmly behind Riel, that they will be fairly represented, that concessions to land claims will be extended, and that the Canadian government acts in good faith. Understanding the importance of this, Riel continues to make strides in his efforts to represent both French and English fairly, forming a convention of forty representatives, twenty from each language group, to discuss Smith's promises and agree on a response. The representatives create a new list of rights, and a delegation is chosen that will head to Ottawa and enter into direct negotiations with Canada. Riel is pleased. His careful planning is working out, and the deaf ears of John A. appear to be opening.

While the Métis prove themselves quite adept at political negotiations, their jailing skills leave something to be desired. Twice in the month of January, big breakouts occur, freeing basically all the leaders of the Canadian Party who so bitterly oppose Riel, including Dr. Schultz, Charles Mair, and the belligerent Thomas Scott. These men ride out in different directions and once again attempt to raise a militia that can violently oppose the actions of the vast majority of Red River, French and English alike. Riel doesn't feel much concern. After all, he has the weight of the people behind him. In an act of goodwill, he orders the rest of the jailed Canadian Party freed in mid-February, on the promise that they will no longer agitate.

Just a couple of days later, Riel's talented horseback scouts detect a large party of armed men apparently heading toward Fort Garry. They alert the rest of Riel's forces, who capture forty-eight men, including the party's leader, Charles Boulton, one of the original surveyors who'd caused so much anguish for the Métis just last year. That a surveyor is attempting to lead an insurrection against the will of the people angers Métis and settlers alike. It's clear to many that the actions of Boulton and the Canadian Party are fuelled by greed for land, land the Red River settlers have rights to since they have lived upon it for so long. Along with Boulton, the belligerent Thomas Scott is once again captured and thrown back into Fort Garry's brig, where his tirades are so bitter and filled with hate that his guards complain repeatedly to their superiors.

The provisional government is now faced with a harsh reality. These agitators are bent on the movement's destruction, and clearly they won't stop. Riel orders the trial of Boulton, and the jury votes in favour of his execution. The message that the Métis must be taken seriously is serious business indeed. When word of this decision reaches Canadian negotiators, they plead with Riel to pardon Boulton. Riel acquiesces. He's not a bloodthirsty man and so agrees to release the surveyor. Boulton, Dr. Schultz, Mair, and the other agitators retreat to Ontario. Riel has no way of knowing that fifteen years later, in 1885, he will face Boulton once again, this time across a battlefield, and that Boulton will be rewarded for his pursuit of Riel by being made a senator.

The ignoramus Thomas Scott, on the other hand, continues to scream out his poison hatred for the Métis, the French, the Catholics, and the Indians from his jail cell. The man is a rabid dog. He hears word that Riel has pardoned Boulton and takes this as an act of extreme weakness, ratcheting up his invective. His guards demand that Scott now be tried, this time for insubordination. And so it goes. Scott is accused and convicted of fighting with his guards, insulting the president, and defying the authority of the provisional government. None of these are capital crimes, so Scott must be shocked to silence when he is sentenced to execution by firing squad. Maybe he hopes for a pardon, and once again the Canadian authorities plead for this. But Riel is adamant this time. The Métis and the provisional government must be taken seriously, and if this means putting to death this poor excuse for a man, then so be it. Scott's jailers have supposedly told Riel that if the provisional government does not kill the prisoner, they will.

On March 4, 1870, Thomas Scott is taken from his cell and into the yard, blindfolded, tied to a post, and executed by firing squad. This action will haunt Riel for the rest of his years.

Despite this setback, just two months and a week later, on May 12, 1870, after direct talks between John A. Macdonald and Métis representatives, the Manitoba Act becomes a reality. Métis grievances are heard, their list of rights is deemed realistic and acceptable, and on July 15, Manitoba is admitted into the Canadian confederation.

While all this plays out on the public and political stage, the original Red River Canadian Party leaders, Dr. Schultz and Charles Mair, are forced to live in exile in Toronto, where they focus their full attention and money on inflaming hatred against the Métis in the Ontario newspapers. They use the execution of Thomas Scott as their rallying cry, and a drawing of an evil-looking Louis Riel shooting a defenceless Scott in the back of the head as he lies prone on the ground with his hands tied behind his back becomes a popular image of the brutality and cowardice of these Métis, despite the fact that the illustration's depiction is so far from the reality.

The influence and political power of Orangemen across Canada, and especially in the halls of Ottawa's Parliament Hill, becomes evident when, despite successful negotiations between the Métis and the federal government, no guarantee for the amnesty of the leaders of the Red River resistance is attained. Riel is forced to view himself as a wanted man, despite his massive popularity in the newly formed province.

In what the Canadian government terms an "errand of peace," a Canadian military expedition led by Colonel Garnet Wolseley is dispatched to Red River in the summer of 1870 for the declared purpose of quelling talk of American expansionism. Ontarians cheer Wolseley's expedition as the suppression of a Métis rebellion. When word reaches Riel that Wolseley approaches in waning August, Riel understands the reality. He faces arrest, imprisonment, and worse. For the second time in his young life, he is made to wander the wilderness, once again returning to Minnesota. Five years later, in 1875, Riel is formally exiled from Canada for five more years. And in the fourteen years between the day he is first forced to flee his homeland and the day Dumont appears in Montana to ask him to return, Riel goes through a transformation that is nothing short of startling.

CHAPTER THREE

Promise

Gabriel has long dreamed of an alliance between Métis and Indians of all nations. What could be more perfect? Now that the buffalo are all but gone, the people are hungry and discontent growls in their bellies. The Cree, Blackfoot, and others have been forced onto the reserves, and many are close to starvation. The Métis' crops this summer of 1884 are poor, and unhappiness settles across the land like a drought.

But Riel's arrival has sparked something, and the news travels fast as a prairie fire that the Father of Manitoba has come here to try to help, to try to make things right. Riel's welcomed as a hero, and large crowds flock to meet him. Gabriel watches as Louis speaks magnanimously at the home of his new host, his cousin Charles Nolin, easily winning over the trust of the Métis, and Gabriel witnesses Louis again a few days later, speaking wisely at a schoolhouse to a group made up largely of English settlers. Gabriel must feel that much more secure in the decision to bring Riel here to help when even the stiff and cautious English, many of whom were Riel's dissenters back in Manitoba, are won over by Louis's words. And if Louis loses some of that English support when he begins to win over the malcontent Indians, then so be it. But in these months of July and August, thanks to Louis's speeches, speeches filled with words of harmony and a future and leadership and abundance and ownership, it seems that some of the ache of hunger, some of the anger at a federal government that won't answer Métis petitions once again, are dulled by this great man's words. Even the Catholic priests nod their heads when they hear Riel speak.

John A. Macdonald, who had been forced to resign due to a railroad scandal, has found himself back in power again, now pushing as hard as ever for a railway that links the east with the west. And his policy of ignoring that which he finds distasteful continues. His deputies have bungled or "misplaced" both Métis petitions and government responses to those petitions, which basically demand once more that the Métis be recognized in the North-West. The bad taste of 1860s Manitoba has returned to the mouths of the Métis, in large part because of a new influx of surveyors and European settlers pouring into the country around Batoche and Saint-Laurent. It seems that the farther west the Métis push in pursuit of their staple food supply—the buffalo—and a life of solitary freedom, it isn't long before these others follow and begin to jostle them for dominance. And so it isn't a surprise that a summer of rather polite demands promises to turn into a winter of outright agitation and defiance of those who don't even have the politeness to respond to repeated letter-writing. All the Métis know that when the railway finally crosses this country, a flood of new settlers will follow. If the government won't accept Métis land claims now, they certainly won't when the new arrivals come to stake *their* claims.

And the land that Batoche and Saint-Laurent lie upon is well worth fighting for. The South Saskatchewan River winds through it, fertilizing already good soil and thick grasses that undulate as far as the eye can see. By the rivers the trees are thick, Manitoba maple and white birch, ash and poplar. In winter the travelling and the hunting are good near the river, and in summer, fishing and some relaxation are mandatory. The Métis have carved a happy existence here, one that spokes out from mass on Sunday and has developed to include farming the land in a serious way now that the buffalo are all but gone. Oh, the buffalo. If not for its slaughter at the hands of the Hudson's Bay Company and railroad developers to feed employees and its absolute destruction down south by the American government in order to bring the Plains Indians to their knees, the Métis could still live the life they were born for, wintering in small settlements and dreaming of the hunt that leads them through the summer prairies.

Gabriel remains the captain of the buffalo hunt, and this role, even though it has been so diminished the last years, commands great respect for a reason. Gabriel is the one who calls the men together in the weeks before the hunt to plot and strategize and try to divine where the buffalo will travel. It's Gabriel who decides the day that the dozens upon dozens of Red River carts creak out onto the plains in a long dusty line, a line that was miles long not so long ago, and it is Gabriel who appoints the scouts who will look for tracks. When the herds are located, it's he who holds council the night before and appoints each man his duty. And what makes Gabriel a great hunt leader is that it is he who rides so skillfully into the stampeding herd and kills the buffalo that he will then give to the sick and the old, the Métis who can't fend for themselves. Gabriel is, in essence, both the military and the political leader of his people. And no one doubts that he is the master of the prairies.

Now though, in 1884, the mixed-bloods find their lot that of small farmers in tight-knit communities, speaking the Michif language, a mixture of French and Cree. The buffalo are so recently departed that the people can still smell their musky hides, the heady scent of blood and entrails from the gutting, the smoky taste of tenderloin cooked over an open fire. But the Métis have accepted that farming the land has now become their mainstay. As much as this realization hurts, it will never stop them from dreaming of the return of the buffalo one day.

The Métis' trials and small victories at Red River, followed by even more government deceit after Riel's banishment, still sting. The Manitoba Act of 1870 that Riel helped create promised the Métis 1,400,000 acres of land, land they'd settled and lived upon for generations. The Métis assumed that they'd choose their lots, most of which nestled along the Red and Assiniboine Rivers. Finally, the people could live in strong communities together with no fear of that land being taken away by outsiders. But John A. hemmed and hawed and eventually decided upon a lottery distribution system, so instead of the choice river lots, those Métis who were lucky enough to win the lottery found that their parcels weren't linked to the rivers at all.

And as Manitoba settled into the fold of Canada, more and more new immigrants came, people from Ontario mixed with Europeans whose own countries no longer wanted them and who spoke so many different and complicated languages. The buffalo continued to head farther west and many Métis decided to follow them, abandoning the fruitless plots doled out by John A. The land speculators swarmed like locusts, buying up these waterless plots from the Métis in deals that were sometimes fair but quite often crooked. Anti-French and Métis sentiment became so strong next door in Ontario that, for the half-breeds, moving away from it began to feel like a good idea. Red River was swallowed by the booming city of Winnipeg, and many Métis craved the old life of wide-open country and just a neighbour or two. For some, their Indian blood whispered to them to follow the dwindling herds, and for others, the idea of freedom came with isolation. And so thousands of Métis, like the buffalo, went west toward the Rockies, drawn to the homeland of their cousins, finding new homes in the towns of Batoche and Saint-Laurent beside lifelong residents of the area like Gabriel Dumont. This was a chance for so many to start anew.

While Gabriel's leadership strength is obvious to all, he recedes this first summer of Riel's arrival. Gabriel isn't a speechmaker, and maybe he understands implicitly that it's best to leave the talking to the ones who are born for it. He is a man of action, and so he withdraws and watches and waits to be called.

With the summer waning, the excitement of Riel's arrival threatens to wane as well. Despite the concerns of the local police and worried bureaucrats like Lawrence Clarke, Ottawa continues to ignore Métis grumblings. A high-ranking federal minister, due to arrive in the North-West in August, ends up a no-show and dashes the Métis' plans of presenting their list of grievances in person to a real-life representative.

Worst of all, Gabriel sees that the priests refuse to take a stand with the people the way they did in 1870. Men like the local priest, Father André, seem afraid to recognize and to speak about what the Métis all seem to know: that once more they face the loss of their homes and of their way of life, a life that they've worked so hard to create. And Gabriel knows that without the support of the priests, the people will be too afraid to make a proper stand. The growing movement is threatened by inaction. Louis's speeches are a welcome thing, but they aren't enough to keep the people focused as they prepare to harvest the poor crops of summer. Gabriel understands that the fire of the pulpit, the fire that propelled the movement of 1869 and 1870, needs to be kindled again.

He finally sees a chance to act in September, when he learns of the visit of Bishop Grandin to the nearby community of Saint-Laurent. Even better, travelling with Grandin are government representatives. Gabriel sees the billiard balls lined up in a potentially exciting way. Take the shot so that

Bishop Grandin is forced to choose action over silence. At the same time, Gabriel and Louis together will present Métis grievances to a federal representative. This will prove to all Métis that the government is indeed in possession of their written concerns. The government will then no longer be able to claim that they are ignorant of the troubles that are beginning to spill over in the North-West, as they've done to date with their silence.

In early September of 1884, Gabriel, although he's uncomfortable with it, gives a short speech in Saint-Laurent to a gathering that includes Bishop Grandin, Father André, and the secretary of Lieutenant Governor Dewdney. Gabriel makes it clear that he's unhappy with the way the men of God have chosen not to involve themselves with the troubles of the Métis. In the Manitoba resistance of 1870, men like Father André were key to the Métis' being not just heard but respected and included in government plans for their country. Gabriel ends his speech, as his biographer Woodcock notes, in a conciliatory manner, asking the priests for guidance. He leaves the political talk to Louis, who immediately follows, and it's Louis who lays out for the priests the demands of the Métis: proper laws regarding the land, better treatment of their brothers, the Indians, and financial dues for the people of the North-West.

As good as Gabriel must feel now that he's active again, it won't be long before his hope for the priests to side with him turns into anger and then resolve. As Woodcock again notes, Bishop Grandin, after a later conversation with Dumont, remarks, "I fear our poor Métis are making mistakes, and that we shall be blamed for it." It soon becomes apparent that the priests don't have the backbone they once did and obvious to Gabriel that the Métis will have to act without them. Louis Riel will now have to fill the role of spiritual adviser. The summer of discontent is officially over. And it's about to give way to an autumn and winter of outright agitation.

CHAPTER FOUR

Secret

Despite Louis's declared intention to return to his quiet life of teaching in Montana in September, he finds himself so popular during this autumn of agitation, so busy meeting with Métis and white settlers and Indian bands, that there's no more talk of his departure. If Louis keeps any lesson close to his heart regarding the resistance of 1869 and 1870, it is that to succeed means to include all. But this is proving even more difficult than it did fifteen years ago. Louis meets with Cree chiefs like Big Bear and Poundmaker whose people are starving on their reserves. The government had promised the Indians who came to the reserves that they'd be taught the transition from a life following the buffalo to a life of farming. Instead, the Indians sit and wait and starve. The spread of disease adds to the troubles, and they are beginning to die in great numbers.

But Louis's conversations with the Indians scare and upset the English Canadian settlers, especially in the heavily white communities of Prince Albert and Fort Carlton just north of

Batoche. After all, the Indian troubles to the south in the U.S. that culminated in the slaughter of General Custer and his Yankee troops are still a living memory. One of the warrior chiefs responsible, Sitting Bull, wasn't he allowed to flee to Canada and live under the noses of the North West Mounted Police? And didn't Riel have powwows with Sitting Bull, that criminal himself, not too long ago? What did they talk about? In fact, what are Riel and that other trouble-maker, Big Bear, talking about now? They are upset with the whites, with the English speakers. They believe that the whites are taking Indian and Métis land, and the full-bloods and half-bloods are certainly acting agitated about their lot. So maybe it isn't the best idea to feed that fire anymore. After all, in the grand scheme of things, we English-speaking, Anglo-Saxon Canadians will always be better off.

But Riel's own people continue to support him. And many of them have no qualms in saying that he does far more than the priests to fight for Métis rights and welfare. Riel asks and receives the blessing of visiting Bishop Grandin to create a new religious society for the Métis with Saint Joseph as the patron saint. On the day in late September that the Métis celebrate this at the church in Batoche, Riel speaks, but not before a number of local priests do. By all accounts the celebration doesn't look like it will be memorable, to say the least, clergy droning on and singing poorly, but Louis saves the day, speaking as eloquently as he ever has, declaring that finally, the Métis are a nation. No one present will ever forget it.

As eloquent as Louis is, he's apparently somewhat tortured internally about a number of things. He still believes that the government owes him a good deal of money for the time and energy he spent in ensuring that Manitoba became a part of Canada fourteen years ago. But he also understands that too much talk of John A. owing him money can come off sounding more than improper, even if it was the prime minister himself who offered Riel $35,000 in the autumn of 1873 as a bribe to leave the country. Now, though, this large sum of cash could come in handy; it could buy the Métis a printing press. The importance of a newspaper for the people doesn't escape Louis. The settlers of Saskatchewan could unite under the paper's banner in reading and writing its columns. What a powerful tool. And of course, some money would also give Louis a little freedom to look after his wife and children properly.

He agrees to a meeting arranged by Father André and David Macdowall, a local bureaucrat, just before Christmas to discuss government remuneration. At this meeting, Father André claims he can arrange for the money to be paid to

Louis. But what appears goodwill on the surface seems to hide deeper and darker machinations on Father André's part. He's become increasingly angered by and jealous of Louis. Riel has eclipsed not only André but all the local priests in popularity and especially in leadership. In the resistance of 1869 and 1870, the priests took such an important role, defending the rights of the Métis and standing front and centre when it came to petition writing and negotiations with the government. But now it's as if they've lost their spines and their drive. None of them offer any real solutions to this repeat of 1869, even though the Métis stare at the precipice of the loss of their land, which will equal the loss of their culture. The priests are French but not Métis, and so maybe they don't understand how deep this concern really runs.

Father André is a tough old man who used to live with and minister to the buffalo hunters, and he makes no bones about not liking Louis. He wants Louis gone from Batoche. In this way, Father André can take control of the Métis again and bring them back to the fold. Louis wants his money. It's owed to him. Father André realizes that if Louis were to accept a large sum of cash, it could be easily spun as his accepting a bribe, and Louis would lose his shine with the people. But all this talk of remuneration and bribes comes to nothing when John A. suddenly reverses past course and claims to be disgusted and surprised at this request for money for Louis Riel. It's political grandstanding at its most shameful. The prime minister, after all, had no qualms in the past about trying to take care of political problems, including Riel, by using hard, cold cash.

The real issue that must torture Louis is not money but this: he keeps a secret, one as hot as the sun. It has given Louis warmth through all those frozen winters spent wandering the wilds as a banished man. Louis knows that he can't keep this secret inside him much longer, and when he eventually shares it with his people, it will release from his chest like a flock of doves. What Louis will soon share is that he has a divine mission, a mission revealed to him by God Himself. Louis Riel has been anointed the prophet of the New World. And his anointed name is David.

In his diaries, Louis seemed to have sensed that Dumont was coming to take him back home for this express purpose. But like any mortal asked by God to do great things, Louis has his occasional doubts. He became an American citizen only a couple of years before, when it seemed as if he could never return home and live without worry of imprisonment or assassination. Louis isn't paranoid about this matter. The premier of Ontario himself had put a $5,000 bounty on Louis's head after the execution of Thomas Scott, and Louis keeps in mind that during his self-imposed and then government-mandated exile, he was elected to parliament three times but never allowed to serve out of a real and rational fear for his freedom and especially for his life.

Louis had made it clear that he'd return to Montana when he'd helped all he could. At first it was going to be September, but that's long past. The decision becomes that much more difficult because the Métis have so graciously, so boisterously taken him in with open arms. Maybe this really is Louis's mission in life, his calling, his path. God made no bones about Louis being a chosen one. God told Louis this Himself a decade ago, near Washington, D.C., of all places, and on a mountain, no less.

Now, though, here in Saskatchewan, this austere country destined to be the new Rome, this fertile ground that's clearly becoming a magnet for men of all nations who wish to live simply and honestly and who don't just mind but are born for the spine-breaking work of the new life, they must know that there's room for them all to live in harmony with their French and English and Indian brothers. Louis has already figured out how the North-West can be divided and shared. This country really is the new world of promise and riches if, and only if, one is willing to live in the agreement that it can be shared by all tribes of humanity, whether they be Scandinavian, Irish, Pole, Indian, or Métis.

In fact, this land of riches shadows the Old World of Europe, the Old World of decay and corruption. The Old World, Rome, is corrupt. And it is dying. Look at these priests like Father André, who is himself from the Old World. He does everything in his power now to prevent the Métis from creating a homeland where all will be welcome and live by the laws of God and of Jesus. Why? Is it so crazy to believe that this land of mixed bloods, of blood from all over the earth, of God's true children, can nourish millions and become the new centre, the new Rome? Why can't it? And why can't Louis's spiritual guru Bishop Bourget become the new pope? Louis doesn't talk about this much, in part because it takes such energy and patience with fools, but this understanding that the Old World is corrupt, a white-washed sepulchre, and that this New World is the future, well it's easy to see. All Louis has to do is sit himself on a bank of the South Saskatchewan River, somewhere close to Gabriel's Crossing on a warm late June day, and watch the puffy white clouds skitter past, the sound of children playing and laughing in French, Cree, English, and Michif, and he knows he's come home, he's arrived home. Home.

But home is always being threatened. Louis, the man with no home, Louis of all people, knows this implicitly. Red River is no longer home and hasn't been for years. It was spoiled when it was digested into the belly of Canada, when

JOSEPH BOYDEN

the Métis were sold out and bought out and Louis was spit out to the south and into Minnesota. This is when the Métis were robbed of their property by the Orangemen wolves.

All that Louis fought for fourteen years ago and lost, though, has presented itself to him again. Now, the same beast that threatened Red River threatens the Métis communities of the South Saskatchewan River. A line must be drawn. This, after all, is the New World. And Louis, by God baptized David, is beginning to more clearly hear the voices that proclaim he is the chosen spiritual geographer of the New World.

With the help of his secretary, Will Jackson, Louis has finally drafted a petition, and it circulates through the Métis and white communities of the North-West during the autumn of 1884. This petition is read, debated, and fought over by them all, and in December, all have agreed it is fair, and it is ready. The petition is sent to Ottawa, a document that's balanced, reasonable, and conservative in its requests. It's the product of months of debate and collective bargaining.

Many months pass before an answer comes back, an answer so brutal to the Métis that the lieutenant governor of the North-West himself doesn't have the heart or the stones to share it with them and so lies about what it actually says.

But in the months of autumn turning to winter while the Métis wait for an answer—or even a simple telegram confirming that their petition has been delivered—they come to realize that once again, John A. Macdonald likes to ignore them. His pleasure in insulting the Métis and the rest of the settlers seems to have no boundaries.

Maybe it is the scorn of the government and the anger of the priests, combined with the newfound pressure of becoming the Métis leader once more, that trigger Louis to begin to reveal his secret. Experts on Riel, including the biographer Maggie Siggins and the American academic Thomas Flanagan, emphasize a heated discussion between Louis and a priest named Father Valentin Végréville in early December of 1884. The day after a wedding celebration during which Louis stays up all night praying on his knees, he runs into the cleric and berates him, insisting that the whole hierarchy of the priesthood right up to archbishop should march with the Métis. It's during this lecture that Louis utters one simple line, but one that carries great weight: "I have a task to accomplish by reason of a divine vocation." A divine vocation? While on the surface these words appear simple enough, for a man already viewed as a rebel and maybe even a heretic by the priests, to actually admit aloud that he believes he is basically on a mission from

God will certainly give them reason to pause. More importantly, Louis's words will provide them with ammunition to use against him.

Also well documented is another, more explosive confrontation between Louis and the clergy just a few days later. This time Louis supposedly confronts a number of priests at once while they are on a retreat. Father André, the same tough old minister to the buffalo hunters and a man so easily angered by even the slightest sign of disrespect toward his rule, is ready with his response. André bellows that Louis is becoming an enemy of the priests and that they will speak against him to all the Métis. To dare question the Church's authority as hotly as he does means Louis is one of three things: a non-believer (which he certainly isn't), a sinner who can be saved (which he might hopefully be), or a heretic most probably under Satan's control (which some priests believe is a real possibility). After the run-in at the retreat, the priests discuss whether Louis, for daring to question their authority and lack of support of the Métis, should face the worst punishment available to the Catholic Church: no more receiving of the sacraments and, as some of the priests present later claim, excommunication as a heretic.

What's been fiercely debated about this whole scenario—and many others in which Louis is the focus—is that so many of the key moments were reported long after they are supposed to have happened, and by people who had plenty of reason to twist them to their liking. The story the priests tell is that when Louis was told he was making enemies of them, he fell to his knees, crying and begging for forgiveness. It was given to him only when he promised never to lead an uprising again. In hindsight, once the uprising actually did occur and everyone around Batoche, holy men included, was on the possible hook, of course it served the priests' best interests to cover their own cassocks. But this might be too simple.

Louis Riel can in no way be understood if his deep faith isn't taken into account. He never utters a negative word against the priests or the church in his diaries. Of course the priests who wrote about this event had grounds to distance themselves as far as possible from Louis when agitation quickly exploded into killing. But this is not the only reason they would paint Riel as an unstable man, a man who's insane. To do so could save not just his soul but also his life during the trial that would decide his fate. When men like Father Fourmond and Father André came to the stand during Riel's trial, his life hung in the balance, and they indeed argued that Riel was insane.

Regardless, when the new year of 1885, the last year of his life, arrives, Louis's ties with the priests, the men who have so shaped and anchored his world, have been severed. And this surely affects everything in his world.

But with the hard times come good times, too. A huge party is thrown in Louis's honour on the first of January, with as many as two hundred members of the Métis community coming together at the home of Baptiste Boyer to celebrate and to show their love and respect for Louis. He has come to make a stand for them, and this party is given in the hope that the rest of the year will be just as bountiful. This will be the year when the government finally pays attention and gives due where due is deserved.

No one at this point can fathom how quickly things will slide into anarchy.

Four weeks later to the day, Dewdney, the lieutenant governor and head of the territorial government of the North-West, receives a telegram from the Halfbreed Land Claims Commission, a commission set up just recently by the federal government. It's a curt response to the Métis petition so painstakingly crafted and debated months before. Dewdney is so taken aback by the commission's telegram that he is shocked into understanding that sharing it with the Métis of the North-West might very well cause open rebellion. Despite the millions upon millions of acres that make up the North-West, this three-man commission sitting in Ottawa has decided that only two hundred of the approximately thirteen hundred Métis who have legitimate claim will receive any entitlement. Anyone who'd received scrip in Manitoba in the past is no longer eligible, regardless of any past impropriety on the part of the government or questionable speculators, and regardless of the fact that the Métis of Manitoba were not given choice parcels of land, land that they themselves had broken with their backs. Virtually nothing that the Métis ask for is broached, including representation in local government, the delineation of all-important river lots, or acknowledgment of Métis rights as a distinct people.

Dewdney hems and haws as to what to do, finally deciding that he'd best gut this telegram to avoid trouble. When it circuitously reaches Louis a full eleven days later, Dewdney has so altered it that it now simply says, "Government has decided to investigate claims of Half Breeds and with that view has already taken preliminary steps."

Word travels fast, and despite Dewdney's fabricated version being far from the answer the Métis hope for, they at least recognize it as a response, finally, from John A. He has received their petition, and it will be difficult for him to not see its simple and inalienable requests.

The excitement of the Métis, their belief that their communal voice has finally been heard by Ottawa, peaks on the evening of February 24. The people have fallen into a near-religious fervour. Prayer marathons for guidance and for leadership, for wisdom and for the future of their people, culminate in Louis speaking to the community at the Batoche church. Louis believes that if he stays any longer, his presence will become a hindrance. It's no secret that John A. is not a fan. Rumours circulate that the police will arrest Louis on sight. The gathered crowd gasps when he announces that it is time for him to return to his simple life teaching in Montana, that the wheels have begun to turn, and it is now best that he step aside so that they may spin freely. The church erupts into cries of disbelief, becoming a single voice of desperation, of pleading that Louis stay and help finish what he has started. Louis sees that he has no choice but to do what they ask. He is moved by their desire, and he is here not only to lead but to serve them. But he warns the gathered crowd that consequences might very well follow. The people, he sees, are willing and able. Consequences be damned. The consequence will be that the Métis will finally have a home. Louis finally has a home.

CHAPTER FIVE

Oath

For Gabriel, these last months through the winter are once again spent standing back in quiet support of Louis, but the brief happiness of February turns into the anger of March. The Métis don't want to accept as normal the manic ups and downs that the government forces them to go through. It's becoming a sickening pattern. If Gabriel didn't know better, he'd swear the politicians were doing this on purpose, setting up the people's hopes just to gut them. Four days into March, the actual words of the telegram to Dewdney and his rewriting of it become public knowledge, and with it, the brutal truth of the matter: only a tiny percentage of Métis will be offered possible title to their land and only after government land agents give their permission. Something in Gabriel hardens forever with this news. He was willing to go the peaceful route of petition, but it has gotten the people nowhere.

Had Gabriel been able to see the bigger picture unfolding—an impossibility for most anyone who didn't have access to all the facts and all the government insider plans in 1885—it might not have been that big of a stretch for him to believe that John A. was actively attempting to incite the Métis to open rebellion by his long stretches of silence followed by short, devastating bursts of antagonistic decision-making that seem to unfairly punish them. Historians such as D.N. Sprague as well as the brilliant comic strip author Chester Brown make a fascinating argument for why it would perfectly serve John A. to incite the Métis to rebellion. John A.'s obsession, after all (an obsession, keep in mind, that forced him to resign because of his direct involvement in a railroad bribery scandal twelve years before), is a railroad that runs from sea to shining sea. But the Canadian Pacific Railway in 1885 is in desperate straits and close to bankruptcy. With the economy in the midst of a depression, Canadians worry that the project has become a fiscal black hole. But what if? What if a rebellion flares up in the west? The insurrection of 1870 is not only still fresh in the minds of English Canadians, it has grown to bogeyman proportions, and anger over the execution of the Orangeman Thomas Scott has never gone away. Riel is back in Canada, fomenting anger in the Métis, and now reports from government spies—including, of all people, Father André and the bureaucrat Lawrence Clarke—claim Riel wishes to pursue his revolutionary agenda even through violent means. And so why not just lead the Métis to water? Why not deny them what they ask for? Get them to act out violently, and what God-fearing Canadian is going to say no to loosening the purse strings in order to get the railroad finished so that troops and supplies can be sent quickly to quash the heathen uprising? Canadians will finally see the railroad's positive use, and John A. will cement his place in the history books.

While this might verge on conspiracy theory, the simple fact of the matter remains that, regardless of whether John A. diabolically planned it or not, the outcome of his poor decisions remains the same. On March 5, the very next day after the federal government's hurtful answer to Métis petitions comes to light, eleven men secretly meet with Gabriel, including Louis Riel. Louis has written a simple oath for the other men that has them agreeing to continue to live in as holy a manner as possible, but it also mentions the taking up of arms if necessary in order to save Métis country from a "wicked" government. The Métis have had enough of being trampled upon, of having their lives dictated to in this wild country by men thousands of miles away. Clearly the time for petitions has passed, and more direct action approaches. Still, Louis himself chooses not to sign this oath—a secret one, of sorts—because he believes his inclusion in any pact beyond the role of a "spiritual leader" will only lead to more troubles for the other men.

Despite Louis's quiet call to take up arms if necessary, it isn't bloodshed that the Métis desire, not at all. The next step, for some, becomes clearer by the day. But it is a dangerous step in that things can certainly escalate to violence if the Métis are not careful. And Gabriel knows violence, especially how quickly normally peaceful men can lose their stomach for it when it is actually upon them. Gabriel, Louis, and the others have to play this particular billiards game with all the skill and cunning they can muster. Talk emerges of a new provisional government, one that fairly represents the people of this land. But there's one major problem, one major difference between March of 1885 and the days of 1869 and 1870: the North-West is now a geographical and political territory of Canada. To try to declare a provisional government when one already exists will be regarded as treason. And with the conviction for treason comes execution. This is a real and dangerous game indeed.

Gabriel knows that the Métis, though, will keep their wits about them. In Dumont's *Memoirs*, years after the uprising, Gabriel notes of this time:

For there is not a more docile people, as disinterested in material goods as the Métis. And I am certain, that if one had given the more cool-headed Métis the alternative of renouncing their rights than winning them through bloodshed, there would not have been a single one of them who would have made the sacrifice; they would have been slightly vexed at first but then would have said cheekily: "Let them keep their rights then! Who needs them anyway!"

Regardless of the desire for most to not turn to violence even as a last resort, tensions run high, and the Métis are devastated to learn of the telegram message that Dewdney tried to hide. News travels fast, even in this lightly populated area. The Métis, yet again, have been forsaken by John A. Macdonald. His government cannot find it in its heart or in its conscience to offer them clear title to the land they've cleared, built homes upon, and settled. All these years of back-breaking work, and for what? For speculators to swarm in once again, selling Métis land literally out from under them to corporations or rich individuals, the government rubbing salt in the wound by offering free land to newly arrived immigrants. How did the Métis become invisible?

Why are they being treated in this way? No one, not the priests or the bureaucrats or the chief factor of Fort Carlton, Lawrence Clarke, dares to answer. To the Canadian government, the rich land upon which the Métis have settled, land that soon will have a railroad running through it followed by the economic boom shortly thereafter, this land is far more valuable than the half-breeds who live on it.

Alas, the Métis are not ignorant, nor are they stupid. The priests and the bureaucrats don't need to say aloud what the situation is. The half-breeds are adept at reading the weather, at knowing which way the wind blows. They are a people of and part of this land. They will not be pushed to act foolishly. This foolishness will be left to another.

The Métis gather at the Saint-Laurent church in large numbers on March 7, when the bad news has settled over the land like more snow. With the support of Gabriel, Louis announces that a provisional government should be created based on the abdication of federal government functions through neglect. Louis has re-worked the petition so recently shot down by Ottawa as a bill of rights for the people with ten straightforward points:

1) That the half-breeds of the North-West Territories be given grants similar to those accorded to the half-breeds of Manitoba by the Act of 1870.

2) That patents be issued to all half-breed and white settlers who have fairly earned the right of possession on their farms.

3) That the provinces of Alberta and Saskatchewan be forthwith organized with legislatures of their own, so that the people may no longer be subjected to the despotism of Mr. Dewdney.

4) That in these new provincial legislatures, while representation according to population shall be the supreme principle, the Métis shall have a fair and reasonable share of representation.

5) That the offices of trust throughout these provinces be given to the residents of the country, as far as practicable, and that we denounce the appointment of disreputable outsiders and repudiate their authority.

6) That this region be administered for the benefit of the actual settler, and not for the advantage of the alien speculator.

7) That better provision be made for the Indians, the parliamentary grant to be increased and lands set apart as an endowment for the establishment of hospitals and schools for the use of whites, half-breeds, and Indians, at such places as the provincial legislatures may determine.

8) That all lawful customs and usages which obtain among the Métis be respected.

9) That the land department of the Dominion government be administered as far as practicable from Winnipeg, so that the settlers may not be compelled as heretofore to go to Ottawa for the settlement of questions in dispute between them and the land commissioner.

10) That the timber regulations be made more liberal, and that the settler be treated as having rights in this country.

Far from being the rebellious, antagonistic, dangerous, revolutionary, and blood-smeared doctrine that men like Lawrence Clarke warned the federal government about, this bill of rights is simple, direct, and incredibly enlightened. Nothing in it, or the similarly worded petition sent the autumn before, asks for anything unfair or beyond the bounds of respectability. When viewed in this light, it becomes quite easy to understand why the Métis became anxious and angry when John A. finally showed his hand.

Gabriel knows that Louis does not want violence, that he detests it. This is proven to all at the meeting when Louis makes it clear that as soon as the federal government addresses the gathered Métis by forming a commission to deal with these respectful demands properly, their newly cobbled provisional government will immediately disband. Gabriel views this as a wise play, and one that all can agree with. The provisional government is simply a tool to help ratchet the tension up enough so that Ottawa will come to the table rather than sending a demeaning telegram.

Accounts of the fateful day of March 17, 1885, vary quite widely, but most agree that a group of Métis riders came upon the chief factor of Fort Carlton, Lawrence Clarke, who claimed he was returning from business in Ottawa. When they asked him if he had any news for them regarding their land claims, he surprised and shocked them when he supposedly spat, "The only answer you will get will be bullets."

What he continued to say, according to Siggins's Riel biography, is that he'd passed an encampment of five hundred policemen who were preparing to arrest the Métis agitators, and they were especially focused on taking Riel. As it turns out, Clarke, for reasons only he could explain, not only greatly exaggerated the number of police, but his false words caused a wave of panic to sweep the Métis communities. As Siggins says of Clarke, "What he accomplished was to jump-start the North-West Rebellion."

Regardless of whether the Métis were already prepared and willing to enter armed resistance, as some historians claim, or whether they were taunted into it by the alarmist and self-serving Clarke, the outcome, once again, remains the same. The Mounted Police have made the first aggressive move. They have shown their hand, or as Gabriel might prefer to think of it, they took the break in this billiards game. This now allows Gabriel the leader to emerge fully in March, and with his expertise as the head of the buffalo hunt, he calls his men to arms and to action. Expecting a large contingent of police to arrive anytime now, Gabriel knows that what his men desperately need are arms and ammunition. Talk spreads of taking Fort Carlton to the north to secure the necessary supplies and a central holdout for the Métis, but unfortunately for Gabriel this doesn't come to fruition despite the very strong possibility that he could have done it.

Instead, Gabriel sends word to the nearby Indian reserves of chiefs Beardy and One Arrow. Gabriel knows he's lost the backing of most if not all English settlers. This became apparent a while ago, especially when Louis introduced the idea of a provisional government and began speaking openly of an armed defence of the homeland. Gabriel believes he doesn't need them anyway. The Indians will help him, and Gabriel's men number in the several hundred. They know this territory as no one else. Gabriel has some nice plans if things indeed turn violent. After all, he has fought for and against his Indian cousins and knows the way of the guerrilla warrior. What he needs most—and worries about most—are those vital arms and ammunition.

With this in mind, he makes his first bold action on March 18. Riding with more than five dozen armed men and his friend Louis at his side, Gabriel enters Batoche and stops in at the store of the English settler Kerr, demanding he hand over guns and ammunition. Not only does Gabriel commandeer a handful of shotguns and rounds, he takes his first prisoners of the insurrection, an Indian agent and his interpreter from One Arrow's reserve. Gabriel realizes that they may come in handy if the time arises for negotiations with the police; he is well versed in prairie warfare and its long tradition of taking prisoners who can act as bargaining chips later on. Many more prisoners will come in the days to follow, and Gabriel will make sure they are treated well even as Louis lectures them repeatedly about his visions and his goals.

From Kerr's, the group heads to the church and deposits Louis there before riding out to cut the transmission wires. The uprising has officially begun, and it will not be telegraphed. Gabriel knows that the less information his enemies have, the better off the Métis will be. After raiding another local, non-Métis store and taking more prisoners, he watches over the next couple of days as his upstart army grows, as Métis from all around arrive in Batoche to throw their hats into the ring.

Gabriel, using his knowledge as leader of the buffalo hunt, organizes this small army of maybe three hundred men into appropriate groups. The best riders will act as scouts, patrolling both banks of the South Saskatchewan River, keeping a sharp eye for the enemy. His next mission is to make a plan to take not only Fort Carlton but the nearby town of Prince Albert as well. In this way, the greatest multi-faceted problem—arms, ammunition, supplies, and food—will be dealt with once and for all, and the Métis will be in a place to wage a guerrilla standoff for months, if need be.

This makes perfect sense in Dumont's closest circle of men, but when Louis gets wind of the plan, he puts his foot down regarding what might end up being unnecessary vio-lence. Gabriel, having been in the position of having to kill or be killed before, is willing to go to the place he implicitly understands is dangerous and where, most likely, men will lose their lives. But during these days when no violence has yet been perpetrated by either side, Louis's strong aversion to it wins the day. On a number of occasions in the near future, Louis's decision to allow the insurrection and the Métis' lit-eral fight for their lives to go only so far ultimately destroys any chances the Métis might have. Gabriel mustn't be happy at all with the call, and tells Louis on a number of occasions that he is giving the enemy too much leeway, but in the end he cannot find it in himself to trust his own gut, for this means going against Louis. The initial problem of a lack of arms and ammunition will grow only more desperate as the weeks pass by.

And so, instead of taking the fort by force, Louis writes the commander there, demanding he give up. Nothing comes of it. Louis, it seems, will go out of his way to avoid bloodshed, but in a rebellion it is bound to come, and indeed, not too long afterward, the dark wings of violence throw a shadow over the country.

As the last week of March arrives, Gabriel's scouts report that they have spotted police across the river and toward Duck Lake. Gabriel knows the strategic importance of Duck Lake: it lies on the trail between Batoche and Fort Carlton, and so whoever controls it can use it as a vantage point, a place to spy on the other. He obtains Louis's okay to raid some stores there and to scout it out more carefully. Once accomplished, that evening Gabriel and his men capture two policemen scouting for Crozier, who commands Fort Carlton. One scout lies and tells Gabriel that he's simply a land surveyor, but Gabriel scoffs at the notion of a surveyor working late at night in the moonlight. The policemen are taken prisoner and, as dawn arrives, with Gabriel and company stabling their horses, a shout goes out that more policemen have appeared.

According to Gabriel, he is slower than some of the others in bridling his horse, and by the time he's done, a few of his men are on their way to meet the police. Gabriel hates not being in the lead and tries to take a shortcut through deep snow, slowing him even further. By the time he catches up to his men, they are in a standoff with the police. Each side numbers approximately thirty, and all are well armed and nervous. Gabriel jumps off his horse, admonishing his own men for not knowing to take this defensive position. That's when he recognizes a Scottish Métis named Thomas McKay who rides with the policemen. Gabriel's shouted insults are hot. He threatens to shoot McKay and makes it clear that he believes McKay is a coward and a turncoat. Gabriel goes so far as to try to strike McKay from his horse with his Winchester, the one he long ago nicknamed *le petit*. But in the scuffle the rifle misfires, almost bringing the standoff to a bloody crescendo. The police, realizing that nothing good can come of this situation, retreat. Gabriel and his men fire a volley over their heads for good measure as the Métis celebrate.

Exhausted, they return to Duck Lake, only to once again hear the shout of yet another police convoy spotted a short time later. As Woodcock points out in his Dumont biography, Crozier, the commander of Fort Carlton, immediately rallies his full strength of troops, fifty-six policemen and fewer than fifty inexperienced volunteers, Lawrence Clarke among them, the troublemaker and instigator demanding that the Métis be taught a swift and painful lesson. Crozier believes that if word of the police's earlier retreat gets out, this will embolden not only the Métis but the neighbouring Indian reserves, and so he acts impetuously, not knowing that at least three hundred Métis have arrived at Duck Lake, including Riel himself.

With his beloved brother Isidore at his side, Gabriel heads out once more to meet the police. This time they've pulled their sleighs off the road and lined them up in a defensive position. Gabriel immediately realizes that the police have come to fight, but still he tells his brother, "We mustn't shoot first; we'll try to take them as prisoners; it's only if they defend themselves that we'll shoot too."

Isidore, carrying a rifle but also a white blanket to show that he means only to talk, and his Cree friend, the wise old chief Assiyiwin, who is unarmed, approach the line of police while Gabriel and his outfit hang back and slyly begin to surround them. Crozier himself, along with another Scottish Métis, this one named Joseph McKay, rides up to meet them. Assiyiwin, seeing how well-armed McKay is, calls him "Grandson" and asks him where he goes with so much weaponry, at the same time reaching his arm out to the younger man. Inexplicably, McKay shoots the unarmed chief dead as Crozier screams for his men to begin firing upon the Métis. Gabriel watches in horror as his own brother is shot dead from his horse. The first blood has been spilled. Gabriel's own blood. There will be no turning back.

Outnumbering the enemy so decisively, and boiling with anger upon witnessing his brother's murder, Gabriel and his marksmen begin picking off the exposed policemen. He later states that he was reloading *le petit* when the police appeared, and that they would retreat once again, realizing that they were outnumbered and nearly surrounded. After a good half hour of men shooting wildly at each other, with Gabriel's troops slowly tightening the noose around the enemy, he senses the crushing defeat the police are about to endure. It's at that time that he spots one of the most striking—and one of the strangest—images of his life. Louis himself has emerged on horseback from the woods behind and trots bravely among the men, completely exposed to police fire, carrying a cross raised above his head, exhorting the Métis: "In the name of God who created us, answer their fire!"

Ever the tactician, even in the heat of battle Gabriel recognizes that the police are going to have to retreat through a clearing, and as they begin to do so, in his own fog of war, not sixty paces away, he exposes himself to too much of their fire. His men watch as Gabriel takes a bullet to the skull and immediately drops, blood gushing from his head. They can only believe that he is dead. His cousin eventually makes his way over to try to see, and as he discovers that Gabriel is alive, that the bullet has ricocheted off his thick buffalo skull (leaving a deep scar for the rest of Gabriel's life), his cousin is shot dead by a retreating policeman. Gabriel has lost two family members in less than an hour.

Gabriel's other brother, Edouard, takes control of the men and is about to deliver the *coup de grâce* by pursuing and killing the rest of the police force when Louis stops him in his tracks, declaring that enough death has happened for one day. Gabriel desperately wants Edouard to go ahead regardless, in part out of retaliation, in part knowing that Fort Carlton, then Prince Albert, and eventually Battleford will fall to the Métis and they will, in essence, control a huge swath of the North-West. Once again the warriors bow their heads to Louis even though their guts tell them not to.

The aftermath of this first battle finds twelve police and militiamen dead and many wounded. The Métis, after witnessing the slaughter of Isidore and Assiyiwin, lose three other men in the fierce fighting. It is a clear victory for the Métis, and Gabriel, tied to his horse and still bleeding profusely from the head, listens as Louis commands a cheer from the men for their brave general.

In this, the first violent uprising in Canada in fifty years, the Canadians of the North-West have suffered their first military loss. Crozier, who attacked instead of waiting for reinforcements that he knew were on their way, is blamed for his foolish decision and berated in reports accordingly.

As for the Métis, they have started on a road they've not taken before, one that they can't turn back from now. Suddenly, the worst possible situation has begun to unfold. Gabriel knows this, knows that the choices have diminished to one: his people must hold off the might and anger of the Canadian military, and the only way to accomplish this will be through guerrilla tactics. This is no longer a billiards game. And more men are going to die before it is over.

CHAPTER SIX

Quickening

A week before blood reddens the snow at Duck Lake, on March 19, Louis instates the provisional government of Saskatchewan. He sees himself as taking on the role of a political and spiritual leader and appoints Gabriel as the adjutant-general who will be in command of the Métis army. Louis has put much thought into what to name the council that will run this nascent government and decides that he must create a new phrase if he's to capture the essence of his vision. He calls this new council the Exovedate, meaning roughly "those who have left the flock." Perhaps his friend Gabriel would have preferred a more masculine name that brought back to life the all-but-vanished buffalo herds rather than the docile and somewhat dumb beasts that a flock suggests, but Louis best understands the Christian symbolism of sheep and departing the fold. The Métis who have gathered around Louis and Gabriel have a difficult time pronouncing—or really understanding—Exovedate, and so they call the new government *le petit provisoire*.

Louis, who believes his health has been pushed to its limit over the now dying winter, begins to feel the exhaustion leaving his body at the telltale signs of spring's approach; the river ice will soon break and the water will surge. Louis's life is like a river. He has been pulled along from his earliest days in a direction that's been preordained. This river, this life, has led him finally here to Batoche, and now he senses the river quickening. The waters are beginning to eddy and swirl, indeed are beginning to froth underneath the winter ice. The power of the river, of Louis's life, pushes hard against the ice that holds it down. This is all preordained, like the seasons, like winter to spring. Soon, very soon, the ice will give with an echoing boom that will be heard clear across the country, across the world, and the water will flow again, free of the ice's constraints.

Louis, feeling the pulse of the river in his veins a few days before installing the Exovedate, makes his boldest public statement to date in front of the Saint-Laurent church. "Rome has fallen!" he declares to the priests and the Métis gathered on the steps of the church which Father Fourmond forbids him to enter. This is the first dove to burst forth from his chest. And the Métis are with Louis now, not with the priests.

More doves follow. It makes perfect sense for Bishop Bourget, the conservative and powerful bishop who has influenced so much of Louis's thinking, to be the first pope of the New World. And so it should be. Rome has rotted from the inside and here, finally, on the soil of the grand North-West, a new Rome can be built. Louis has many more specific plans, from renaming the days of the week to praying for the resurrection of a dead American politician who will help the Métis cause, but first he must deal with the most daunting of issues: forcing John A. to recognize that the Métis have fair claim to the lands upon which they live.

Louis believes that *all* he wants is realistic, but there are those who have labelled him mentally unsound in the past. Indeed, he spent almost two years in an insane asylum for behaviour that those who care for and love him couldn't understand. They couldn't grasp that God spoke to Louis on the mountain near Washington, D.C., during the days he attempted to hold secret court with American president Ulysses S. Grant, during those days when Louis firmly believed nothing short of an American military invasion of western Canada could help secure a real Métis homeland.

Yes, Rome has fallen, and Bishop Bourget is the perfect man to become the new pope. Ten years before, Bourget himself sent a letter confirming Louis's deep-seated belief that his path was a righteous and important one. Ten years ago, in July of 1875, Louis was deep in the wilderness of his soul, officially banned from Canada, a bounty on his head. The Orangemen clamoured for his assassination in a year when he had already been elected to the Parliament in Ottawa by the people of Manitoba but could not claim his seat. It was a year of torment and true suffering, made worse in that he was separated from his large and beloved family. But a letter from the bishop helped quell some of the pain, for the letter stated what Louis already knew. The bishop wrote, "I have the deep-seated conviction that you will receive in this life, and sooner than you think, the reward for all your mental sacrifices.... For He has given you a mission which you must fulfill in all respects."

Five months after receiving that letter, while in the American capital and attending mass not long before Christmas, Louis was struck by an overpowering mystical experience. He writes in his journal,

> I suddenly felt in my heart a joy which took such possession of me that to hide from my neighbors the smile on my face I had to unfold my handkerchief and hold it with my hand over my mouth and cheeks. In spite of my precautions a young

boy about ten years old, who was a little in front
of me, saw my great joy.... And if it had not been
for the great efforts I made to restrain my sighs,
my tears and cries would have made a terrible
noise within the church.

Over the next while, visions continued to visit Louis,
including one where the spirit of God comes to him, filling
Louis with a divine light before transporting him to what he
understands to be the fourth heaven, where he is instructed
for at least an hour and a half about the nations of the earth.
The visions culminate in a powerful one while Louis hikes
up a mountain near Washington, D.C., the same spirit who
visited Moses "in the midst of cloud and flame" appearing to
Louis. It says to him in Latin, "Rise, Louis David Riel, you
have a mission to accomplish for the benefit of humanity."

Understandably, Louis's friends are somewhat concerned.
Louis takes to referring to himself as Louis "David" now,
even though David is not his given name. More than that,
he sinks into horrible places where he shouts and bellows,
sometimes even in church, and most odd of all, a couple of
times he tears his clothes from his body and rips them to rib-
bons, claiming that God wants us to be naked in front of
Him, for it shows we have nothing to hide.

Louis is certainly beginning to understand that he has a mission to fulfill, and it's becoming clearer to him that he is a prophet of the New World, but family and friends can't quite wrap their heads around this. Within a year of receiving his visions, out of concern for his mental well-being, Louis is spirited back into Canada to Montreal, where he is placed in the care of his uncle. But the man soon realizes he can't do enough for his nephew after Louis, among other tantrums and strange behaviours, has an embarrassing outburst during mass, and so Louis is committed to an asylum just outside of Montreal. He's admitted in March 1876, under the pseudonym Louis R. David, but not long after the doctors, fearing he will be discovered and captured by the authorities, move him to another asylum near Quebec City. This time, Louis enters the asylum under the name Louis Larochelle.

And so Louis spends twenty-two months under the care of doctors who are impressed by his intelligence and his great knowledge of philosophy, Christianity, and Judaism, one by the name of Dr. Howard even going so far as to comment that he's never quite sure if Louis's grandiose talk isn't acting rather than actual hallucinations. And while Louis continues to have irrational outbursts, the rest seems to do him well. He continues his religious exploration through his writing, composing theological tracts that attempt to explain his stance, his hopes, and his vision. In late January of 1878, Louis is finally released with the stern warning to lead a quiet life. He tried, didn't he? But his mission was reawakened when Gabriel called on him, back in Montana, months ago, what feels here in March of 1885 like years ago. And so Louis finds himself in Batoche, on the verge of creating the New World he'd so long imagined.

Now, though, there's no denying that blood stains the snow at Duck Lake. The Canadians fired first and left the Métis no other option but to defend themselves. It's not at all too late to try to hammer out a fair truce, a just solution, for his people. The government should be amazed that this truce actually held for so long, for fifteen years, since the Red River resistance. For this is how Louis has seen the last decade and a half: as only a truce. The government has never properly dealt with the Métis situation. But now they'll have to, won't they?

Louis has told Gabriel and the others that the British are tying themselves up with a war overseas and that the chances of British troops coming here are slim. He reminds Gabriel and the others how long it took, months and months after the Red River provisional government was created, before the Canadian troops even threatened to arrive. What Louis does not take into account is that even though great swaths of the Canadian Pacific Railway lie incomplete between here and Ontario, great lengths of it are finished, and the Canadians have no intention of letting things slide. News of the battle of Duck Lake has spread rapidly, and the clamour for Louis's head across English-speaking Canada is growing as fast as only hatred can grow. Already more than three thousand troops and volunteers are heading here from Ontario to join up with the two thousand police and volunteers in the North-West. In the next weeks, that number will grow to eight thousand men.

News of the Métis victory doesn't travel only to the whites. Indians on reserves across the North-West take the news with mixed reactions. Some see joining the bearded holy man and his tough war chief as a sure way to end up in an even worse place than the one they're in now. All Indians know the vicious savagery a white government will bring down upon red people who dare try to protect themselves. The ghost dance movement is still a few years away, a desperate last chance for some prairie peoples to stave off their own destruction, but already so many Indians recognize the misery of their situation. Others are far too proud to consider joining forces with a group they have a difficult time considering themselves part of and understand that patience is a very important part of Indian life. Besides, who is this Riel who preaches of the god of the whites and dismisses the old ways?

But important men do seem to share the same vision as Louis: that the government must be forced if it is to be fair. The Cree leader Big Bear, who was the last to accept reserve life and its restrictions just a few years before, and Poundmaker, the peace-loving chief whose young warriors push hard against patience, watch as their people starve, their young men growing restless and speaking with the anger that comes when your loved ones grow skinny with sickness.

Just one week before, Louis and Gabriel had shown that you can stand up to the police, to the authority of the government and win, and some young Cree men begin to allow this to fill their bellies. Big Bear pleads with his warriors to not act rashly, but one of his war chiefs, Wandering Spirit, has gained a voice among the young and angry. All of them, fed up with the position they find themselves in, break away from Big Bear and enter the community of Frog Lake, taking hostage the Indian agent Thomas Quinn in his home before dawn on the morning of April 2. Quinn, who treats the Cree with arrogance, is a tall man whom the Cree see as short. He's become the focus of their anger because of his harshness and his racist world view. Against his father's wishes, Imasees,

Big Bear's younger son, is among the party. They take more prisoners as the morning progresses and begin to occupy the village, gathering the locals in the church.

Before noon on this fateful morning, Wandering Spirit orders the prisoners moved to an encampment outside of town. Quinn is stupid enough to try to fight this decision, and in the ensuing argument Wandering Spirit shoots him in the head. Panic follows, and the Indians begin shooting. When the smoke clears eight more men lie dead, including two priests, one of their lay assistants, and local businessmen. With the remaining villagers functioning as his prisoners, Wandering Spirit and his group take Fort Pitt. News of an Indian uprising out west only feeds the flames, and General Frederick Middleton, in charge of the expedition to crush it, uses this latest violence, forever after termed the Frog Lake Massacre, to keep his soldiers pushing west at a brisk pace.

The violence of Frog Lake is exactly what Louis abhors, and yet he struggles to understand that his desire for the Indians to join forces with the Métis will certainly lead to killing. He remains convinced that things have not gone too far for the government to sit down at the table, despite Gabriel's not being shy in telling him that he gives every advantage to the enemy by not allowing guerrilla tactics.

Louis continues to hold his ground, telling the Métis that the Lord speaks through him, and that the outcome of all this will be positive. The doves, they continue to escape from his chest.

At this point, as the first week of April draws to a close, the Exovedate moves back from Duck Lake to Batoche, basically taking over the village. The most important date of the Catholic calendar, Easter Sunday, arrives, and Louis, along with many of his supporters, attends a mass given by Father Moulin. As the priest gives his sermon on the importance of the Métis' obedience to the clergy and to the government, Louis is able to remain silent, but after mass he can no longer contain himself and chastises Father Moulin for his refusal to support the Métis cause. Moulin calls Louis a heretic, and if there were any confusion among those in earshot as to how wide the split between Louis and the priests is, it's certainly clear now.

The next day, Easter Monday, General Middleton and his army, having crawled their way through the worst of the breaks in the CPR in northern Ontario, set into motion his plan of attack. Middleton divides his army into three: Major-General T.B. Strange will pursue Big Bear and Wandering Spirit via the North Saskatchewan River; Lieutenant-Colonel Otter will head to Battleford, where the population hides in the fort, fearful of the Indian uprising and Chief Poundmaker's warriors, who sacked their village; and Middleton will attack Batoche and deal with the madman Riel.

Middleton marches from Qu'Appelle with just a little over four hundred men, and within a week will find himself only a hundred miles from Batoche. He has no plans whatsoever to enter into negotiations with the traitor. Middleton prepares to bring the full weight of the law onto the Métis' heads instead.

Gabriel, he knows this, but how to convince Louis?

CHAPTER SEVEN

Decimation

Gabriel knows what he must do to win this war that has started. For that is what it now is. Gabriel has excellent scouts and an excellent communications system of fast horsemen. He even has a friend who is serving as a freighter for General Middleton's army, and all tell him that forces approach at a speed Louis did not think possible. Poor Louis. He is a great spiritual man, but not a great military strategist. This army doesn't approach in order to sit down at the table and talk. They are coming to fight.

Thankfully, it's already become apparent that many of the Canadian soldiers are green volunteers who, it appears, have never even camped outside. The army wears bright red tunics that can be spotted from miles away, and like any large force, it marches in a noisy column that makes it difficult to manoeuvre through some of the thicker river bush of aspen and willow and poplar. Gabriel and his people know this area well, though, and know when to hit and when to run. But Louis refuses to allow Gabriel to go on the offensive, using every excuse he can muster: what about the police in Prince Albert? They might attack if they hear that Batoche is lightly guarded. But the most nonsensical of all is that guerrilla tactics are too much like Indian tactics, which means that they are too savage. Louis worries that if Gabriel and his men fire into Middleton's camps at night, they might accidentally kill Québécois volunteers. Gabriel, though he would never say anything against Louis in public, must feel himself to be at wit's end.

But Gabriel doesn't like second-guessing himself, which is what he's been doing. Does he do this simply because he can't read or write and Louis can? Gabriel knows how to deal with the Métis; he understands their culture and politics. What he fears, what he's always feared, is that he doesn't understand the workings of the Canadians, of their politicians. But Louis does. He's already changed the course of the country's history once. And so Gabriel won't question Louis's actions and decisions anymore. Louis understands, obviously, in a way that Gabriel can't.

This is what Gabriel could do if he were allowed to act, or if he shrugged off Louis's decisions and acted regardless: he and his horsemen would ride southeast, the way the army will be coming, destroying railway tracks and especially bridges along the way. This will slow down Middleton

hugely by causing chaos for his supply teams and reinforcements, but will especially cause severe stress for his green
troops, who will realize that they are now cut off from civilization to the south, that it is suddenly just them versus the
savage Métis and Indians. Gabriel creates plans to constantly
engage the camps with gunfire and raids at night, causing
even more stress. As he says in his own words, "I am sure we
should have made them so edgy that at the end of three
nights they would have been at each other's throats."
Preventing soldiers from sleeping is classic guerrilla warfare
that works, and Gabriel knows it. Just as important,
Gabriel's plans include the raiding of supply trains and
depots. The headache that will not go away, however, is that
Gabriel's men, despite being great and willing shots, are
sorely under-equipped.

In his memoirs, Gabriel explains why he agrees to listen
to Louis and goes against his own gut: "I yielded to Riel's
judgment although I was convinced that, from a humane
standpoint, mine was the better plan; but I had confidence
in his faith and his prayers, and that God would listen to
him." Gabriel has, in the end, been won over by Louis's
faith. There must be a grand design, and Gabriel, who is a
hunter and a man of action, makes the decision, for now
anyway, to put his trust, indeed his life, in the hands of the

mystic. But with each passing day that Middleton's army marches closer, Gabriel watches as his own men begin to allow anxiety to eat away at them. Gabriel understands that to sit idle can destroy resolve. And worst of all, with each passing day of inaction, his small and poor army's chances of success become more and more impossible.

Finally, on April 23, more than four agonizing weeks of waiting since the battle at Duck Lake, Gabriel's head wound far from healed and the intense pain causing him to sometimes pass out if he coughs too hard, his scouts bring word that Middleton's army has camped only six miles south of Fish Creek, the same place where just eight months ago Gabriel, with Louis and family in tow and freshly arrived from Montana, was treated to a hero's welcome. General Middleton wanders freely on Métis land and Gabriel and his captains sit here uselessly? This is the final straw. Gabriel confronts Louis, informing him that he plans to ride immediately and attack Middleton's camp by night.

"Very well! Do as you wish!" Louis snaps, and, upon short reflection, adds that he will accompany Gabriel and his men. Louis now shares with Gabriel his great fear that Gabriel is not healed well enough yet, and that if something happens to him it will be a deadly blow to the Métis. Gabriel knows that this type of concern, as kind as it is, has no place in a military confrontation. He's been held back long enough; the time to strike has come and gone numerous times. Maybe, just maybe, if he strikes hard enough at Fish Creek, a perfect place for an ambush, it won't be too late. But time is of the essence. Gabriel must start the twenty-six-mile journey now if he hopes to use the night's cover for an attack.

Gabriel immediately sees the effect of waiting so long on his men's courage and drive. He's able to leave just thirty men behind in the charge of his brother Edouard to protect Batoche and rides out with fewer than two hundred, a mixed group of Métis, Saulteaux, Cree, and Sioux. Along the way Gabriel chomps at the bit while Louis has the men stop numerous times so that they might pray the rosary with him, slowing the group even further. By midnight, after killing and consuming two of a local farmer's cows, the men are full and exhausted. Scouts approach, informing Gabriel that mounted police have planned a sneak attack on Batoche from a different road and that Gabriel's brother Edouard is requesting an additional thirty men to return and help protect the town. Gabriel doesn't believe the police will be doing this at all, but he's somewhat relieved to allow Louis to return with thirty of the men Gabriel will least need. He is not happy, though, to find that almost all his men want to go with Louis to Batoche. They aren't afraid of Middleton and his army, they say; they fear for their families' safety and wish to be close to protect them. Gabriel reassures them, and the ragged army continues to Fish Creek.

With dawn quickly approaching, Gabriel divides up his diminished force and gives strict word to obey his commands. Do not ride upon the trail. Scouts will see your horses' hooves and be alerted. Do not burn a fire. It will be seen, and smelled, for miles. Stay silent and alert.

Gabriel orders the majority of his force to hide along game paths on Fish Creek, which runs east from the South Saskatchewan River, carving a forty-foot deep ravine into the earth. But he cannot keep track of all of them, especially some of the younger ones with cotton in their ears. The Canadians will have to pass by here and try to cut across the creek. And they will most certainly be following this road, which leads straight to Gabriel's house on the river only twenty miles away. The bush is thick and easy to hide in, and despite the typical thinking that having the high ground is always best, Gabriel does the exact opposite. His men, hidden below in the ravine, will easily spot Middleton's army backlit by the sun, as big as the easiest targets the Métis have ever shot at. And the ravine's dense bush offers excellent cover. Most important, Middleton's two cannons, which he's dragged behind him for thousands of miles, will be useless at such an angle, trying to fire down on the Métis below. Even a bad shot will be able to pick off the artillerymen as they try to load.

Once Gabriel has given his strict orders to the 130 men in the ravine, he heads south a short way to a coulee with twenty horsemen. His plan is an old prairie tactic, and Gabriel knows it will work if he keeps the surprise. Gabriel and the others hide themselves in the dense brush. They will watch the Canadians pass and then, when Gabriel's main force engages the Canadians at Fish Creek, Gabriel and his riders will ambush them from behind, closing his trap on Middleton's men. Gabriel calls this tactic his buffalo pound, carefully orchestrated to lead the animals into a long and narrow natural pen where escape becomes impossible, before picking them off, one by one.

But once Gabriel has left with the horsemen, a few foolish young Métis and Indians disobey his orders and chase a couple of cows along the road for sport, leaving notice of their presence for any sharp-eyed scout to see. And indeed, just after dawn, a wily little group of English half-breeds hired by Middleton to do exactly this kind of work spot the fresh hoofprints and race back to sound the alarm.

Gabriel himself only makes matters worse. Soon after he and the horsemen go into hiding in the coulee, Gabriel spots a lone Canadian scout approaching. In his obsession to gather as many arms and ammunition as he can, as well as count coup, he tells his men that he will chase this scout and club him off his horse and take his weapons. Gabriel clearly doesn't want to shoot him, for firing *le petit* will surely alarm the Canadians. He brashly rushes off to pursue the scout, and as he chases him out of the coulee, a Métis horseman in a good viewing position shouts that a group of forty lie just beyond the bend. Gabriel's ruse is up and he's just lost the vital tool of surprise. He shoots the man he's pursuing and turns just in time to avoid the enemy's volley.

But they in turn pursue him, and Gabriel rushes back to the relative safety of the brush and the others. In the ensuing gun battle he loses one or two riders to wounds but holds off the group, which ends up fleeing back to the bigger force. Gabriel and his men have managed to hold off a force twice his size. But now he faces, without his greatest tactical weapon of surprise, an army that by day's end is ten times his size, trying not just to hold off that army but to force it into retreat.

When Gabriel and his horsemen sneak back into the Fish Creek ravine, to his anger and shock he finds that not even fifty of the original force of 137 still remain. At the simple sound of gunfire, his army is abandoning him, disintegrating in front of his eyes. Instead of panicking, Gabriel refocuses his men through example, and as the first orderly column of Middleton's troops present themselves in a neat line, silhouetted on the ridge above, the Métis below begin to cut them down. Middleton orders his men to hold firm and for the cannons to come forward, but just as Gabriel has predicted, the big guns are useless at such an angle, not able to fire their shells almost straight down at the Métis, who are mostly hidden only fifty or sixty yards away. Fearing big losses of his own men and having no idea of Gabriel's strength but estimating it at five times its actual size, Middleton makes no major decisions for a number of hours, simply trying to hold the higher ground as his men are slowly picked off by Métis snipers.

All day, almost four hundred of Middleton's men have been trying to come to his aid by crossing the river, but unfortunately they have only one scow to contend with the freezing and swift-flowing torrent chocked with ice. But they do begin dribbling in, and Middleton continues to try to send a few new waves of soldiers to try to break the Métis' backs.

The Métis are desperately low on ammunition and men. Many had only twenty rounds at the outset of battle. But they shoot carefully and with great skill. No shots are wasted. This doesn't take care of the biggest problem: Gabriel knows that although Middleton can easily overrun him any minute, he hasn't yet because he fears Gabriel's force is much larger than it really is. Gabriel needs back those fifty or so men who rode off last night. He sends off couriers with word to bring reinforcements with God's speed and faster. By afternoon, Gabriel himself has only seven rounds left in *le petit*'s belly. He prays that more of his men will come, and come fast.

Despite their rather grave predicament, the Métis are in high spirits as the battle and the afternoon wear on. Middleton's troops are indeed untested. If Gabriel commanded so big and well-equipped a force, the battle would have been over hours ago. Indeed, he wouldn't have let himself get into such a position. To keep his spirits up, Gabriel shouts out to those who can hear him, "Don't be afraid of bullets! They won't hurt you!" His men laugh at the silliness, but Gabriel's wounded head aches so badly that he fears it will explode. Neither he nor his men have had anything to eat since dawn, and now the day is growing long. He can assume that Middleton's men haven't either. Gabriel's men break into various French songs, taunting the English above them.

Gabriel has one more trick up his sleeve, another old prairie ruse. His reinforcements from Batoche have still not arrived, and Gabriel has to maintain the impression of a large force. With night a few hours away now, Middleton will surely attempt one more hard push to overrun the Métis, and he will most probably succeed, especially when the Canadians discover how tiny a force is actually holding them off. Gabriel's lost more men to casualties and desertion over the course of the day, and in this late afternoon, the tiny bit of daylight warmth turning to cold and threatening sleet and rain, he makes his gamble, ordering his men to light on fire the prairie grasses between them and Middleton. The wind is in Gabriel's favour, and the fire spreads. Wet from the morning rain, it burns low and smoky. Gabriel orders a number of his men to advance through the blaze and fire on the surprised Canadians before they have a chance to go on the offensive. He makes it clear that they should pick up every enemy rifle and round they can find. Gabriel hopes this minor offensive will cause enough confusion in the Canadian ranks for them to panic, and they do, but not enough to go into full retreat.

Gabriel's trusted brother Edouard and eighty men finally arrive from Batoche not long before dusk, thus ensuring that Middleton won't be able to flank Gabriel's men in the ravine. As night falls it becomes too dark to see the enemy, and with both sides dehydrated and brutally hungry, Middleton begins to pull back his forces. Gabriel has done something astounding in holding them off. Much later, when he is asked how many men he thinks he shot that day, he answers simply, "I couldn't have missed many."

When the dead and wounded are counted, the number, by most standards of battle, isn't high, but it speaks of the accuracy of Métis fire and the cruel efficiency of Gabriel's tactics. He's lost four men this day, with two wounded. But the small Métis force has inflicted fifty casualties upon Middleton's forces, with ten killed. Basically, one in ten of Middleton's soldiers are wounded or dead, a literal decimation. He's stunned by this, as are his men, and it takes two weeks for them to lick their wounds and wait for reinforcements.

Gabriel, head pounding, barely makes it back to Batoche in his own saddle. But he does. Many of his men are forced to walk the long way home. More than fifty Métis horses were slaughtered in the ravine today, their large bodies picked off by Middleton's soldiers.

Having not just seen but battled the enemy that Louis "David" now calls Goliath, Gabriel can only wish that he'd acted much earlier and against his friend's demands. Goliath is certainly real. And when news reaches the Canadians that they've been handed a second defeat, Goliath will certainly come full on.

CHAPTER EIGHT

Ordained

While Gabriel and his men fight General Middleton at Fish Creek, the battle waging all day, Louis fights his own battle back in Batoche. He fervently prays hour after hour, kneeling with his arms outstretched, petitioning God and His son, begging the Virgin Mary and Saint John the Baptist, patron of the Québécois, as well as Saint Joseph, newly minted saint of the Métis, to protect all his people, to protect Gabriel and the other brave soldiers, and especially to protect the women, the children, and the old ones of Batoche and surrounding areas. When Louis's arms grow tired, he implores the women around him to help hold them up. Word arrives in the early afternoon that Gabriel needs more men desperately. Louis doesn't want the ones who rode back with him last night and who now guard Batoche to leave, but Gabriel's brother scoffs at this. He will not see his dear Gabriel die alone at the hands of the English. The force meant to protect Batoche gallops off, and Louis prays harder that these defenceless ones around him are not now surprise-attacked by the serpent that is the Canadian military.

Body shaking from exertion, Louis knows that through prayer he's helped usher in a victory for the Métis. When Gabriel and his men return, exhausted but happy, Louis is ecstatic. In order to thank the Lord properly, Louis declares four days of fasting. He hopes to purify his people for the upcoming struggles. For the next days he keeps a thorough diary, seeking answers and feverishly praying to God that Middleton not become the victor, that his cannon be broken into three, and that the Métis understand that the loss of fifty-five horses at Fish Creek, a horrible blow, is God punishing them for their love of gambling on the animals in races. Louis believes it is a small price to pay in that so few Métis lives were lost on the battlefield.

Louis, in these days following Fish Creek, finds much solace in defining his new church. The new church is, literally, a freshly built, rough-hewn log structure in a willow copse near town, since the priests who run the church in Batoche no longer get along with Louis or want him there. He knows that priests are simply instruments of God, and that instruments often break. Those men are certainly broken, and it's Louis's place now to construct the new church. He knows that hell cannot last forever, for this goes directly against God's divine mercy. Eventually all sinners will end up in heaven, reconciled with the creator.

Louis replaces the fallen priests with his own ministry consisting of members of the Exovedate. Each is given some of the important holy obligations of the church: the ability to administer the sacraments, the ability to hear confession. Gabriel and the others are now, basically, priests. They must scratch their heads over this newest turn of events. From here on out they will have to be on their best behaviour.

Louis's decision to change the names of the days of the week now that the new Rome is rising makes good sense to him. Using the old names is akin to worshipping false idols, and so Louis renames Monday, Christ Aurore; Tuesday, Vierge Aurore; Wednesday, Joseph Aube; Thursday, Dieu Aurore; Friday, Deuil Aurore; Saturday, Calme Aurore; and Sunday, Vive Aurore. His fascination with the Old Testament allows him to change the Sabbath from Sunday to Saturday. With General Middleton and the Canadian army at their doorstep, the Métis around Louis don't appear overly concerned with his innovations, or interested, really. There are much more pressing issues.

The priests of the area, though, are frightened and furious. Their people have taken up arms. Killing has begun. The villages are in anarchy. The priests are being ignored by the majority. There will be hell to pay. They finally do, on April 30, what some say they should have done a long time ago. Louis is officially excommunicated, along with all of his followers. The priests can stand for this no longer. Order must be restored at any cost, and if this means, in the near future, giving information about Métis strength—and weaknesses—to General Middleton, then so be it. What's most important is that the Canadian government and the Church in Rome clearly understand that the priests of the North-West have nothing to do with this rebellion. Louis, rather than exploding in anger when he hears the news, answers quite calmly, "Priests have been ordained to support the spirit of religion. Priests are not religion."

Louis doesn't pin his hopes on these priests. He pins his hopes on something else entirely: Louis still believes that John A. will sit down at the table and make a deal with him to treat the Métis fairly and with respect. Surely the people of Canada, even the Protestant Orangemen, see that what the Métis ask for is fair and just. Surely they will see that the police fired first back at Duck Lake and rode against the Métis at Fish Creek. It's not too late to find peace and to find fairness in that peace. Louis writes in his diary on April 29, just five days after Middleton's routing at Fish Creek:

O my God, for the love of Jesus, Mary, Joseph and Saint John the Baptist, grant me the favour of speedily reaching a good arrangement, a good arrangement with the Dominion of Canada. Oh, mercifully arrange everything that this may be. Guide me, help me to secure for the Métis and Indians all the advantages which can now be obtained through negotiations.

Grant us the grace to make as good a treaty as Your charitable and divine protection and favourable circumstances will permit. Make Canada consent to pay me the indemnity which is my due, not a small indemnity but an indemnity which will be just and equitable before you and men!

LOUIS STILL HOPES BEYOND HOPE for a peaceful end to all of this for the Métis, the Indians, and himself. That he still holds out for John A.'s payment of what he believes he is due certainly speaks to Louis's desperate desire for some kind of security, a real promise that he might have a sane and simple future. This provisional government will not last and is not meant to be looked upon as an act of treason. It has been created to force John A. to enter negotiations, and as soon as he does, the government will be disbanded. But just as importantly, Louis is asking that this battle—a battle he's fought all his adult life—be recognized by the Canadians as truly just.

As each day passes and April turns into May, and as Middleton's army reorganizes and plots to crush the Métis, half-breeds continue to trickle in from the farms out on the land. They bring stories of how Middleton's men have destroyed everything, burning homes and stealing all the livestock, leaving the French and Michif speakers with nothing but the clothes on their backs. Middleton has no reason to do this. He is making this into a war between not just the Métis and the Canadians, but also the French and the English. Of all the people in Canada who watch this rebellion unfold in the newspapers, the only other ones who are in any way sympathetic to the Métis are the Québécois. Canada's future relations with the Québécois will be deeply affected by the actions, and inaction, of the next few months.

CHAPTER NINE

Goliath

Gabriel knows that he, not Louis, truly understands the gravity of what they've allowed to happen. Middleton has marched to within miles of Batoche, and despite the Métis bruising them badly not once but twice, the next battle will be decisive. Middleton has spent the last two weeks licking his wounds while encamped at Fish Creek. Gabriel has been forced to begin preparations for the defence of Batoche, something he should never have had to resort to. His guerrilla tactics would have slowed Middleton to a stop, and within months John A. would have had his hand forced politically to make a deal and negotiate with the half-breeds. Hell, Gabriel could have staved off the Canadians till next winter and let the prairie cold destroy the green, city-dwelling Protestant troops. But it is Gabriel who's allowed this to happen—his men digging rifle pits on the town's edges and the women and children digging caves into the banks of the South Saskatchewan River—because he did not argue fervently enough with Louis. Louis is a prophet, and

JOSEPH BOYDEN

Gabriel will not complain about what has passed and what he cannot change. The quickest route to defeat is in mourning what can't be undone or worse, allowing it to weaken you like consumption. Louis has promised that God will listen to the Métis' pleas for justice, and Gabriel knows to put his faith in Him. Dumont has changed in this last year. Louis has given him a focus and a newfound understanding for that which is holy.

If Gabriel knew how troubled Middleton and his men are—the Canadians are hunkered down near Fish Creek, many of them fearful for their lives in this foreign land—he might have pushed beyond his night harassments. Middleton didn't take into account how to deal with his wounded and is forced to try to create a field ambulance from nothing. He writes to Ottawa that the war skills of the Métis in that first confrontation were such that he is lucky his whole army wasn't slaughtered. He also realizes that his troops' initial rush to join in order to crush heathens has turned into something quite different now that they are on the Métis' doorstep. The government's propaganda—that evil Riel and his hordes are bent on the destruction of the commonwealth—was not at all borne out as the troops came into contact with farmers and families fearing for their lives, or encountered abandoned farmhouses, livestock still grazing the fields and clothes still in drawers, as the people fled the approaching army. These Métis live a tough but honourable life of backbreaking work. This much is clear from the simple, clean farms. It doesn't stop many of the troops from ransacking them, though. After all, this is war. And even Middleton gets in on the action, collecting some of the finest pelts he can and shipping them back east. But to most of his men, it's clear that these western people are not at all the animals they've been painted to be.

Regardless, they have begun open rebellion, and open rebellion must be crushed. On May 7, Middleton finally feels confident enough to begin a slow and careful march along the South Saskatchewan River toward Batoche with 850 soldiers and a 150 wagon–long line of supplies. Teams of horses pull four cannons and an American Gatling gun, a deadly weapon for the time that sprays an unending fire of large-calibre lead at the enemy. All of this is arrayed against fewer than two hundred poorly armed and equipped Métis hiding in rifle pits dug less than two feet into the ground. Gabriel prays that the miracle Louis speaks of will come to fruition. Apparently, it won't come in the form of Indian allies. Poundmaker and his men are busy routing and defeating the contingent of Canadian soldiers sent to squash him near Battleford, but, like Riel, he doesn't have the stomach for a full-on slaughter of the Canadian troops, even when the possibility presents itself.

What Gabriel probably doesn't know is that a group of reporters from back east travels with Middleton and his army, reporting every move to the hungry masses who devour Ontario newspapers. This is not just a first test for the young country's military against an enemy—an enemy from within, no less—it's also the first time that the Canadian media travels embedded with its troops. Gabriel and Louis are becoming more and more infamous with every headline demonizing or romanticizing them in turn. One day the Métis fighters are snivelling cowards, the next marksmen and horsemen of such skill that surely more troops will soon be needed.

Soon after Middleton breaks camp, his troops begin looting and burning every farmhouse they come across, regardless of whether it is Métis or white-owned. The troops take special pleasure in demolishing the house they find sitting at Gabriel's Crossing. It is thinly but nicely furnished and contains two oddities: a foot-powered clothes washing machine and, most interesting, a full-size handcrafted billiards table. After a few games they dismantle it and haul it away before burning down Gabriel's home.

Middleton understands that word will spread as quickly as fire that nothing in his army's wake will be left standing. It's a message to the Métis, most of them women and children, who cower and wait in Batoche for what must feel like the approaching apocalypse. While Middleton forges his path of destruction, he also remains extremely wary and even fearful of Métis prowess. Twice they've whipped Canadian troops, and a third whipping will prove devastating. His plan is simple. It's a two-pronged manoeuvre, and the first—and only—naval attack on the Canadian prairies. The steamer *Northcote* slowly plies its way down the Saskatchewan River, weaving its way around sandbars and crawling through the constantly shifting shallows. Middleton has ordered it fortified with wooden armour against Métis rifle fire and stocked it with Canadian troops and artillery. It drags two barges of armaments and supplies behind it. Middleton believes that word of the approach of the steamer will draw a large number of Métis out of their fortifications and down to the river to attack it. And that's when his main army will sweep in from the south, overrunning Batoche quickly. If all goes as planned, the battle will be won within hours.

But Middleton is so cautious in his advance on Batoche early on the morning of May 9 that the steamer arrives a full hour early, and Métis scouts announce its approach. Gabriel himself rides down to the bank and orders his marksmen to fire on it from both sides of the river. He sees that the *Northcote* is clearly well armed and it pulls barges of sorely needed resources. As his men fire from the two banks, Gabriel dashes along the river on horseback, shouting for his men to drop the ferry line at Batoche landing. The heavy cable will rip the top half right off the steamer and with any luck, it will then ground itself in the shallows where Gabriel and his men can pirate away much-needed supplies.

Gabriel watches as the cable is lowered just in time, grazing the pilothouse and ripping off the smokestacks, sparks and ash pouring out, which in turn starts a fire on deck. But the steamer, no longer under power, spins around a sandbar and drifts off uselessly for two more miles downstream before it catches and holds on a spit, too far for Gabriel to plunder it, but also too far away to be any use to General Middleton.

When Middleton finally comes within eyesight of Batoche, word of the *Northcote*'s fate reaches him. His surprise two-pronged attack has been nullified. He takes the high ground of the rise, placing cannon and the Gatling gun upon it, and begins firing at the houses in town, civilians be damned.

In his desire to take the *Northcote*, Gabriel is too late in using a time-honoured plains warfare tactic of setting the prairie grasses on fire in the path of the invaders. The long stretch of *la belle prairie* on the outskirts of Batoche is left unscathed but for the trampling of humans and of horses and wagons. Gabriel doesn't worry about this too much. It would prove only a minor setback for the approaching Canadians anyway, despite its being a fine chance for Métis marksmen to take down some of the weepy-eyed soldiers. He awaits the miracle of which his friend and prophet speaks.

Early on in this first day of battle, a group of Métis sees the chance to take a Canadian field gun and rush the position. The inexperienced Canadian troops almost flee, but their officer rallies them and turns the Métis back with fire from the Gatling gun. The Métis slip back into their well-camouflaged rifle pits, so carefully constructed that many of Middleton's troops have no idea where they are positioned. The day plays out into a stalemate of wasted gunfire, the Métis firing lightly, the Canadians in useless barrages. Cannons set a number of houses on fire, and the dreaded Gatling gun's rat-tat-tat keeps the heads of the Métis low.

Beyond the crippling of the steamer *Northcote,* the most stunning event of the day occurs when a white flag appears at the church door; the Métis watch one of the priests,

Father Moulin, emerge when the firing stops and march directly to the Canadian troops to confer with Middleton. Whispers travel that the priest has surrendered. But more than this, he has taken the side of the Canadians. He has become a traitor, giving away the positions of Métis rifle pits, field strength and weaknesses, and especially their lack of ammunition and food. To add to the insult, Father Végréville also abandons his people and shares vital and damning information with the general. For the Métis who fight for their land and way of life, the priests have most certainly betrayed them. This day and this action inflict a wound that never heals.

Well before nightfall, General Middleton orders his troops to withdraw to a hastily constructed stockade at a nearby farm. Although the day's casualties are light, Middleton knows how the approaching darkness will certainly work against his troops, offering the sneaky Métis opportunity to pick them off in large numbers. While Middleton is willing to burn down homesteads, loot property for personal gain, and fire cannon and small arms onto homes where frightened women and children cower, he subscribes to the strange nineteenth-century notion that gentleman soldiers do not fight after dark.

But it's this type of guerrilla warfare that Gabriel excels at. All night his men fire into Middleton's camp, their war whoops and animal screams keeping the soldiers awake and afraid. The Métis try to scare the hobbled horses into a panic, and the constant fearful whinnying adds to the terror. Few of the Canadian redcoats are able to doze, never mind sleep, and when reveille is called the next morning at 5 A.M., the men are exhausted and nervous. To worsen their misery, the night has been cold, falling below freezing, and the sun's full but weak May heat is still hours away.

Just before noon on the second day of battle, with the Canadians trying to push back to the position near the church they'd reached the day before, Gabriel sets the prairie grasses on each side of them on fire. The Canadians, nervous in the acrid smoke, watch with stinging eyes as a few of their men are picked off by Métis marksmen. Captain A.L. Howard, the American with the Gatling gun, finds that his weapon is near useless when he can't see the well-hidden Métis, some of whom are not more than thirty yards away. Instead, he settles on ripping apart the cabins in town as Canadian cannons focus on trying to destroy the rest. They are mostly successful, and few structures are left standing by the end of the second day.

Why Howard, this American from Connecticut, a career military man with no quarrel with the half-breeds, is trying to kill them in large numbers confuses and angers Gabriel and the others.

It turns out that Howard is not acting as a representative of the American military, nor, supposedly, of the Gatling company. Both organizations deny sending him. He's volunteered himself and this new weapon to the Canadians. As Joseph Howard (no relation) explains in his wonderful depiction of the Métis in *Strange Empire,* the Gatling gunner is here because he regards himself as a scientist, a scientist who's had no real chance to test and analyze this new deadly weapon that he's fallen in love with. Sure, he's tried it against bands of hit-and-run Indians, but not in a battle scenario such as this with two opposing sides in set defences against one another. The Battle of Batoche is proving the first real testing ground for the Yankee from Connecticut and his murderous weapon. The drumbeat sound of Howard's machine gun as he cranks the handle deftly, spraying hundreds of rounds in mere minutes and ripping apart cabins, is as much a psychological weapon as a physical one. The Métis realize that they are up against a force that is far superior in equipment and numbers and especially in technology. In fact, a number of Métis are armed with old shotguns or single-shot muskets that are unwieldy to reload, and that's if they have any ammunition left. Many of the men are already out of real bullets and now, on just the second day of battle, are forced to load their ancient guns with nails, old buttons from their jackets, even stones. *Please, Louis,* Gabriel prays, *show us the miracle you'd promised would come.* If any miracle happens on this Sunday, it's that for a second full day the Métis in their shallow rifle pits are able not just to hold off but to absolutely confuse and stymie a force nearly five times its size, actually pushing them back a good distance from the church they'd so handily taken the day before. General Middleton is confused and angry. He at once fears the loss of his men to wily Métis hunters and is driven near mad that such a small force of desperate half-breeds continues to prove so difficult to crush.

Once again, well before sunset on this second day, Howard's Gatling protects the Canadian troops as they try to retreat to the relative safety of their stockade, but many of the soldiers are caught out in the open field near the church and two are killed by Métis marksmen. While the numbers of dead and wounded remain low on the Canadian side, the Métis continue to inflict their own psychological damage on the redcoats. Their hit-and-run tactics are working.

On this second night, the Canadians sleep a little better. All day they'd laboured on strengthening their compound with earthworks, and the arrival of even more wagons and supplies makes them begin to feel invincible. Gabriel decides that his ammunition supply is too low to engage in another overnight campaign of terror, and so the Canadians are able to light fires and eat their first hot meal in two days before retiring.

Monday drags out much the same as Sunday had. Gabriel expertly moves his men, undetected, throughout the fields and gullies from rifle pit to rifle pit; to save ammunition the Métis fire lightly, but in such a way that Middleton is convinced the priests were wrong about how many men are really hiding like wild animals in their shallow dens.

Gabriel sends out one more desperate plea to Poundmaker and his warriors, begging them to join the Métis. If he could speak face-to-face with Poundmaker right now, he'd say, *Look! We have held off their force all weekend. If you join us now, it will not be too late. Together we can send the Canadians back east with their tails between their legs. We can reclaim our freedoms and you will never be told again to live on a reserve and to dig in the earth for subsistence. A new day approaches. Join us.*

Poundmaker, nervous about entering into such direct conflict but impressed by the Métis' ability to defend, finally breaks camp and begins to move toward Batoche. His men hold many different opinions of this action, from belief in its destructive folly to exaltation at the prospect of old freedoms returning. Poundmaker moves across the prairie with a slow determination. He will not be rushed to foolhardy action. Gabriel worries that the Cree chief travels too slowly. He also knows that something is very close to breaking, and most certainly that break will come tomorrow.

Gabriel hears word on Tuesday morning that Louis, holding the same cross he carried at Duck Lake, announced something odd to the congregation gathered in a grove by the river just as dawn broke: that if the skies today are clear, the Métis will be successful and will be saved. But Louis's vision also revealed that if clouds cover the sun, the Métis will be doomed. Gabriel peers up from his foxhole and sunlight blinds him, falling warmly on his shoulders. *Louis, you are an odd man, but a holy one. What other choice do I now have but to believe your strange words?*

General Middleton's officers have finally convinced him that the last days' lack of success means a new strategy needs to be tried. Middleton's fear of an all-out attack is that his men will be slaughtered and he will in turn lose all credibility as a commander. He thinks he's found a middle ground that will ensure success. Again, it is a two-pronged attack, this time strictly by land. One of his officers, Lieutenant-Colonel Van Straubenzie, will command a central force, the majority of the nine hundred soldiers now gathered at Batoche. Middleton will take a hundred and fifty men, a cannon, and the Gatling gun and ride in a wide sweep around Gabriel's northeast flank. The hope is that Middleton's ride will serve as a diversion and Gabriel will send most of his forces to protect against it. That is when Middleton will fire a large volley as a signal to Van Straubenzie, who will then charge in with his much greater force and rout the Métis once and for all.

To what appears to be Middleton's great surprise, everything goes as planned. He sees Gabriel rushing his men to Middleton's flank. Gabriel has been waiting for this action for days, it turns out. Knowing that Middleton's numbers were so much greater than his own, Gabriel's been confused as to why a sweeping action such as this didn't happen earlier. His northeast side has been the weakest all along. Gabriel's been fooled by Middleton for the first time, believing the general to be in control of the majority of his forces, and now Gabriel leaves his midsection perilously unguarded. Middleton excitedly commands his soldiers to fire their signal shots to Van Straubenzie, but the wind has picked up so strongly that Van Straubenzie doesn't hear the volley. Believing that Middleton has failed, Van Straubenzie sits patiently with his force, leaving Middleton confused and, eventually, in a great rage. Disgusted at his main force's lack of a response, Middleton rides off dejectedly to lunch. He feels a fool, and for good reason. A perfect opportunity has been lost.

While Middleton grumpily eats his lunch in the protection of the stockade, one of his officers, Lieutenant-Colonel Williams of the Midland Battalion of Port Hope, Ontario, sickened with frustration at the lack of proper generalship and recognizing the Métis' weakened position, commands his battalion to charge straight down the middle. His men rise up as one, and with a great shout, charge the Métis rifle pits, many of them empty or manned by old men firing nails from shotguns. Within a half hour Williams has the Métis in full retreat, the sunshine of the day gone now and a light rain falling, the darkness Louis had spoken of this morning that signals the destruction of his people.

Gabriel falls back to the river, and with the water at his back and a small group of maybe eight men, he holds off a force of dozens of Canadians for nearly a half hour. But eventually he, too, must flee. There's no soldier alive who can find him once he decides to go into hiding in the surrounding countryside. Gabriel knows this much is true. But it gives him little comfort now that he sees defeat, and Louis's miracle, so far, hasn't arrived. Gabriel knows, deep inside, that it never will. Some of his braver men retreat to the town and hide in what buildings remain, fighting off the Canadians as long as they can before they are either killed, flee, or are roughly captured.

And so this is how the Battle of Batoche, the last stand of the Métis, ends—not with a bang but a whimper. Old man Joseph Ouellette, aged ninety-three years, is one of the last Métis to die, bayoneted to death by an overzealous young Canadian soldier as he lies defenceless in his rifle pit. Another Métis, this one a ten-year-old girl named Marcile Gratton, is killed by a stray Canadian bullet while trying to find her mother. The Métis that Gabriel had ordered to protect the northeast flank disappear into the woods, and few prisoners are taken this last afternoon. The women and children cowering in caves in the riverbank hear word of the collapse of Métis resistance, but it will take another day or two of near starvation and near freezing to death at night before they begin to trickle out and surrender to the Canadians. They throw themselves upon the mercy of Middleton and the others.

With little organization, the Métis defenders melt into the surrounding plains and woods by the river, confused now as to what they should do. They, too, begin to surrender in dribs and drabs, unsure whether they will be executed on sight. But Gabriel knows this much: he will never surrender to Middleton, and he will never be captured, either. He spends the next three days brazenly riding and sneaking through the adjacent prairies, ravines, and coulees, searching for his dear friend Louis. Gabriel knows he has fled as well and hides somewhere nearby, praying and asking God's mercy for his people at the hands of the victorious Canadians.

Gabriel never finds Louis, but he does find Louis's wife, Marguerite, and their two children. Like the other women and children, they are starving and cold, and so Gabriel spirits them to his father's house. There, his father instructs Gabriel that he must leave: the angry Canadians will surely kill him if they find him. At first Gabriel refuses to listen to this talk; he can still serve a purpose by helping to feed and hide the Métis who won't surrender. But even Gabriel's beloved Madeleine urges him to flee, and he begins to realize he has no other option. Finally he agrees, and begins the long journey to the only safe place he can think of: the wild country of Montana in the United States. Gabriel lights out with his old friend, Michel Dumas, but even as they leave Batoche he is planning to raise a small force of Métis to perform a daring rescue of Louis, who surely must soon surrender.

In all, about twenty-five souls lose their lives in the Battle of Batoche—not many at all by the horrific standards that would be set in the First World War a few decades hence, but plenty for a battle that should not have happened. The Métis resistance has been crushed. Homes are wrecked or burned down, the people hide in the woods like animals or give themselves up to the Canadian army, and Gabriel's dream of a secure and prosperous homeland vanishes with him into the wilderness. What of Louis? Gabriel wonders as he rides away. What has happened to the prophet of the New World?

CHAPTER TEN

Wilderness

On the afternoon that Batoche falls and the Métis are scattered, Louis is once more cast into the wilderness. But the pain of this particular suffering is so acute that he wonders if death isn't the only option now. It would be simple enough to die. As simple as walking out of the poplar by the river where he hides on this day that he has lost everything, as simple as showing his bearded face to the first Canadian soldier he sees. Surely there'll be no mercy for him.

A few hours ago Louis watched in horror as the sun disappeared behind dark clouds while afternoon came. God spoke his decision. The Métis will perish at His hand now. They are being crushed. Louis must question if he has gone too far this time. Has he angered God by being so bold as to speak out loud that Rome has fallen and the new Rome will rise right here in the Canadian prairies? Has he gone too far in denouncing the inaction of the priests when it came to the sacred rights of the Métis? Has he gone too far in allowing himself to be called a prophet, the prophet of the New World?

Louis still has the letter from Bishop Bourget telling him that he is meant for important things. But it strikes him now as he listens to the last of the Métis skirmishing in town with the redcoats—the women and children wailing in their holes in the riverbank, the dying half-breeds crying out for water in their foxholes—that maybe he was meant to lead his people to destruction, not salvation.

The darkest night of his life begins as the rifle fire from town peters out and the crying of women and children turns into moans. Louis kneels and prays, begs God to show him some sign. But on this first night, nothing comes. Only the sounds of men whispering as they quietly slip through the woods and the shouts of victorious Canadians up in town.

The next day the Canadian patrols swarm over the land, and many Métis fighters realize that it might be best to surrender and throw themselves on the mercy of Middleton. Word begins trickling out that the general is confiscating all weapons. With most farms in shambles the men need their guns to hunt for food, but this clearly will no longer be an option. What other choice is there but to surrender? Food supplies are gone and the women and children are hungry. The trickle turns into a steady stream of wretched half-breeds holding white handkerchiefs and giving themselves up to redcoat patrols.

Moïse Ouellette, the son of the ancient Joseph who was bayonetted mercilessly the day before, delivers a letter from Middleton to Louis. Middleton states that Louis will receive safe passage to the Canadian camp, where he will be offered protection until John A. decides what to do with him.

Louis answers that he needs more time to reflect, pray, and write before he will turn himself in. He retreats to his hideout and asks God once again to light a path for him. He's heard that Gabriel is searching for him. One option is for the two of them to slip through the Canadian lines and make a run back to Montana. But can Louis do this? How can he abandon his people and, like a coward, slip away into the night? Louis doesn't hold it against Gabriel if this is what he must do. Just today word came that Gabriel had killed a couple more Canadian soldiers while collecting blankets and provisions for his people. Gabriel literally has blood on his hands, and so he must flee or be killed.

And then the answer strikes Louis like a lightning bolt. Yes! Suddenly he knows exactly what he must do! God has finally spoken, and as always, God's word is exact. Louis will turn himself in to Middleton. He will tell Middleton that now that the leader of the rebellion has been captured, he must offer leniency to all Métis in the country. The pressure will be taken off his people in the short term.

But what about the long term? What can be salvaged? God proves his greatness once more when Louis is struck a second time by a lightning bolt. Surely he will be taken to trial for what the Canadians call a crime. And won't a trial attract huge attention? Louis can imagine that a trial for treason will garner not just national but international attention. A phoenix can rise from the ashes of Batoche. It can. Louis will make sure that he's given a platform from which he can espouse the simple, just, and fair requests of the Métis. Louis will turn himself in and use the trial that follows to continue pursuing the dream of a Métis homeland in the vast Canadian wilderness.

On the afternoon of May 15, just three days after the fall of Batoche, with his dear Marguerite and children cared for by friends, Louis walks out of the bush and along a path near Guardepuis Crossing. He's tied a white handkerchief on one sleeve and holds the letter from General Middleton in his hand. It doesn't take long for a small patrol to see him and order him to halt. When they ask him who he is and he answers "Louis 'David' Riel," they can't believe their luck. Surely there will be a bonus for finding the leader of the rebellion! They happily take him into custody and hurry him to General Middleton's camp.

Despite the attempt to bring Louis into the camp secretly, word spreads fast that the leader of the rebellion has finally surrendered. Louis sits in General Middleton's tent and swarms of officers and reporters arrive to get a glimpse. Louis still fears for his safety, especially at the hands of the soldiers in the camp, but Middleton once again promises that he won't be harmed. The two chat for a long while, and Middleton asks Louis how he possibly imagined he might defeat such a large force of soldiers. Louis responds that the hope was never to win so much as to hold them off until the Dominion understood it needed to deal with Métis concerns directly and through negotiation.

Middleton orders a tent pitched for Louis beside his own, and for the next number of days, while they await word of where Louis will be taken, they speak of many things. Often they double back to the battle and the wish of both men that it could have been avoided.

Within a couple of days Middleton is instructed to bring Louis to Regina, where he is to stand trial. On the day before he is to leave, a military photographer captures a haunting image of Louis. The photo shows him in silhouette, standing in front of a tent, wearing a Stetson and the heavy wool pants of his people. Louis's beard is full and unkempt, as if he has given up grooming. His posture, not quite straight, suggests his weariness. He still wears the white armband of surrender on his left arm, and the soldiers behind him can't help but stare. The prophet of the New World, to one who might not recognize him, looks like any hard-working and hard-living member of the Métis community of Batoche. But this man who stands here in front of a military tent, he is not from here, and this place is no longer his home. Once more, Louis has been cast into the wilderness.

CHAPTER ELEVEN

Crossing

For eleven days Gabriel and his friend Michel Dumas ride through the Canadian wilderness of Saskatchewan, south to the freedom of Montana. What would normally be a three-hundred-mile journey doubles in length as the two men are forced to avoid the obvious trails that now swarm with Canadian soldiers and scouts, all of them looking for the master of the prairies. Gabriel knows the first long section of his ride from childhood memory, but as he approaches Montana, he must recall the trip he made less than a year ago, when he first went down to ask Louis to come back to Batoche with him.

Does Gabriel regret bringing Louis to Saskatchewan? Does he regret not fighting harder with the prophet about waging a guerrilla war? It isn't in Gabriel's makeup to regret. That which has happened has already happened, and nothing he does can possibly change it. Long before he brought Louis back from exile, the Métis were heading for a battle with the federal government. Maybe Louis served to speed up the process. But it would have come, regardless. What Gabriel does still have control over is what he can do in the next weeks, the next months. He will attempt to rally any Métis and Indians he can find who are willing to join him, and he will make a daring rescue of Louis. The battle for a Métis homeland is not over. It will never be over as long as Métis live in the North-West.

As if to prove his point, Gabriel continues to come across small bands of Métis and Indians who are sympathetic to his cause. They feed him and point out the best trails. Resting during the day, riding from dusk to dawn, and praying to the Virgin Mary for guidance, he crosses into the U.S. when he fords the Milk River. Now it is Gabriel who is the home-less one, a man exiled from his own beloved family and country. He'd told Madeleine he would send for her when he found a temporary place of safety in which to settle, but until then, he doesn't feel whole.

As good as Gabriel was at escaping the Canadian army, his luck runs out shortly after he crosses into the States. Gabriel and Michel are surprised by a U.S. Army patrol and are taken to Fort Assinniboine in Montana. As George Woodcock points out in his biography of Dumont, the com-mander of the fort, when he realizes just who it is he has in his custody, quickly concludes that this is a political, not a military, issue. He wires to his commander who wires to his, and the hot potato that is Gabriel Dumont makes himself known all the way to the president of the United States, Grover Cleveland. Cleveland sees that the Canadians haven't asked for Gabriel's extradition and realizes that John A. has enough on his plate trying to deal with that strange man Riel, and so he orders Gabriel and his friend freed, even welcomed to wander around the country as they see fit.

After a comfortable stay at Fort Assinniboine, where he's treated more as a celebrity than a prisoner, Gabriel makes his way to Spring Creek, Montana, where he has a brother-in-law and there's a strong Métis community. From there he begins to visit other communities in Montana, trying to gauge whether he can raise a group of men who are willing to ride with him back to Canada and free Louis. But every week more and more reports confirm that Louis is so well protected that it will take an army to free him. What was at best a grandiose idea begins to wither on the vine. Gabriel, so far from home and stuck now in this foreign country, begins to realize his idea is nothing more than a silly dream. He will have to try to find other means to free his friend.

The guilt, now, of abandoning his friend, his family, his people, and his country begins to torture Gabriel. After all, he's never run from a fight in his life, even when he was

JOSEPH BOYDEN

heavily outnumbered and even when death appeared to be the sure result. But isn't this exactly what he's just done? Gabriel makes it known through the newspapers in Montana that he was solely responsible for the violence that broke out in Saskatchewan and that Louis had always been for peace.

Gabriel finds out that Louis has been taken to Regina, where he is to stand trial for high treason. Gabriel, through his channels, lets Louis's lawyers know that he wants to serve as a witness at the trial, that he wants to once and for all clarify that he was the general and it was he who led the troops. Louis was simply a spiritual adviser who never even fired a weapon. What court can sentence a man to death for carrying a golden crucifix? Gabriel has finally figured out a true way to help the prophet. Louis's lawyers, in the few days of preparation they have before the trial, work feverishly to get the Crown to agree to allow Gabriel safe passage to Canada. This is Gabriel's one real chance to help Louis, and he waits anxiously for word that he can safely return home.

CHAPTER TWELVE

Words

Louis's confinement in his tent beside General Middleton is quite civil. But when it comes time, during the third week of May, to be taken to Regina, the feeling of safety that Louis has been lulled into begins to disappear. He boards the *Northcote,* the same steamer that Gabriel disabled and came close to capturing on the first day of the Battle of Batoche. On board are a number of wounded Canadian soldiers, and when they hear that the madman himself is along for the ride, they become hostile. A constant guard is posted to Louis, not so much to prevent his escape as to protect him from armed and angry soldiers.

Louis does find some solace in a young officer who has been assigned constant watch over him. His name is Captain George Young, and for the next eight days, he becomes a sounding board for Louis. Their conversations range over many topics, but Louis is smart enough to always return to Métis grievances and the reasons they were forced into conflict with the Canadian government. If this Captain Young is a spy planted to glean Crown evidence from Louis, he will not get it. In their conversations, Louis learns that the man's father, a Methodist minister, is actually an old compatriot from Red River—in fact, quite astoundingly, he is the man who led the rabble-rouser Thomas Scott to his execution upon Louis's orders. And now, Louis must wonder, does the son lead another man to his death?

When the *Northcote* ends its voyage at Saskatoon, Louis and Captain Young are taken by cart over rutted and rough terrain to Moose Jaw. Word has spread that Gabriel plans to attempt to free Louis and the going is slow and cautious. The dozens of heavily armed soldiers accompanying the cart are fearful that every grove of trees or clump of brush harbours expert marksmen waiting to pick them off. But the trip is uneventful, and when they arrive in Moose Jaw Louis is whisked by train to Regina, where he's to stand trial.

If conditions with General Middleton were civil, Louis's two-month stay awaiting trial is abysmal. A detachment of Mounties is now in charge of him, and the men's disdain, even hatred, is obvious. They are English-speaking Protestants, many of them belonging to the Orange Order, and there's no sympathy in their bones for a Catholic half-breed agitator and murderer like Louis Riel. He is locked in a small, stone cell, his leg chained to the wall. His meals consist of potatoes with a few stringy bits of beef. The place is cold and dank at night, and hot and claustrophobic during the day. Louis's only exercise is kept to short walks, during which he is forced to carry the heavy metal ball that is attached to his chain. He's given a pen and paper, though, his only solace. Louis writes poems and reflections, and asks the Mountie in charge that his wife and children be looked after. While political prisoners should be handled with more respect than this, Louis's spirit sinks when he realizes that he's being viewed as the lowest common felon. He's truly in the hands of the enemy now, and any hope that he'd be treated with the equality and respect his people deserve dissolves in the growing late-spring heat.

Information about and access to the outside world is kept from him, which only adds to his sense of doom. What he doesn't know is that a number of Quebec Liberals, many of them old friends and allies, are rallying to his defence and starting a fund for him. They are able to hire four respected lawyers: François-Xavier Lemieux, Charles Fitzpatrick, James Greenshields, and T.C. Johnstone. The thinking is that Louis will need both French and English lawyers so that the trial isn't too easily viewed as an English–French battle, a majority versus minority issue. In many ways this will be a trial about the future of all of Canada, and Louis's defence team will symbolize this. Louis needs help from all corners if he's to stand a chance.

His lawyers have a few options. First and foremost, they want to change the charge against Louis from high treason to treason-felony. In the case of treason-felony, the presiding judge and jury are given complete discretion as to punishment, which can range from a few days in prison to life. But the other charge, high treason, carries only one penalty: death by hanging. There are solid arguments for why Louis should be charged with the former rather than the latter; there is plenty of set precedent for this charge, and besides, Louis is an American citizen, having become one not long before Gabriel found him in Montana. How can he be charged with high treason, then, when he isn't even a subject of the Queen? His lawyers, though, are not novices, nor are they naive. The Crown is out for blood, so the chances of the lesser charge being applied are minimal.

There are other options. One is to begin to plan a defence claiming that Louis's rebellion was justified and a product of acute and continued federal mishandling and even criminal ignorance of Métis petitions for land claim review. But this route is complicated, time-consuming, and dangerous. The chances of getting a sympathetic hearing from a jury likely composed mainly of English-speaking Orangeman are slim at best.

The option that quickly becomes most useful is to pursue the obvious: Louis Riel is not guilty by reason of insanity. It's no secret that he spent a long time in different asylums in the 1870s. His writings are laced with what are clearly insane ramblings. He has acted in countless bizarre ways over the course of the rebellion, including stating his belief that he is a prophet of the New World. He's even taken on the Biblical name "David." It would be far easier to convince a jury—even a hostile one—that the man is insane. This will at the very least spare him from the gallows.

After six weeks languishing in his tiny jail cell, Louis, with little knowledge of what his lawyers are thinking or even when they might arrive so that he can meet them, is taken to the courthouse in Regina a few miles from his jail cell. Still fearing that the warrior Gabriel Dumont will stage a daring rescue, the Mounties go to strange lengths to foil such an attempt, dressing Louis up as a policeman and sitting him in a wagon for his first ride to court, with three real policemen at his side. It's a large and daunting caravan, and Gabriel, hundreds of miles away, is unaware of the stir he continues to cause.

According to the court system, Louis must be charged with an actual crime by someone called a claimant. For reasons that remain murky, the man chosen to be the claimant is the police chief of Hamilton, Ontario, a town thousands of miles away. In what seems for Louis another sure sign that he's doomed, this police chief is a member of the Orange Order. Louis is charged with high treason—waging war on representatives of the Queen's government. As Louis knows only too well, death by hanging awaits upon conviction.

Louis is very smart, but he has no legal training. When he finds out that the acting judge will be a man named Hugh Richardson, he has even more reason for deep concern. Richardson is not a judge in the proper sense. He's what's called a stipendiary magistrate, a barrister of at least five years' experience who serves as a part-time judge in the thinly populated North-West Territories. Stipendiary magistrates are hired by the administration in Ottawa, an administration that holds no love for Louis; their job is to help ease the duties of the few, overworked real judges in the area. Louis must wonder why a full-time judge isn't assigned to sit on what should be regarded as an important trial. Worse, he finds out that Mr. Richardson, yet another Orangeman, served as counsel for the territorial governor in 1880 and once wrote a letter to the Ministry of the Interior strongly condemning the Métis leaders as "evil influences" doing "no good" for the half-breeds.

Louis must also be distressed to learn that, rather than the typical twelve jurors, with its greater chance to find empathetic men among that number, a trial under a stipendiary magistrate requires only six jurors.

Louis's lawyers are nine days away from arriving, and Richardson has scheduled the trial to begin on July 20, which means they will have only a few days to prepare. What more can possibly be stacked against him? As it turns out, plenty. When the jury is eventually selected, all six are white, English, and Protestant. When Louis's lawyers move to have the trial taken to Winnipeg, where Louis might find a little sympathy, the judge quickly shuts them down. Louis Riel will face trial in hostile Regina, and his fate will be decided by a judge and six men who have very little in common with the Métis, who in fact have more interest in crushing the half-breed movement.

On July 15, five days before the trial is to begin, Louis's lawyers finally arrive in Regina. The one hotel in town is already filled with reporters and the curious, so the first night the lawyers are forced to sleep on a floor. In what can only be called a media scrum, Louis meets his defenders in front of a group of clamouring reporters. He immediately expresses how happy he is to see that these men represent different languages, nationalities, and religions. Louis, as always, firmly believes that inclusion, not exclusion, is what wins the day. For the first time in a very long time, he doesn't feel quite so alone anymore, quite so vulnerable and in the dark. But this is not to last long.

On July 20 Louis and his lawyers appear in the courtroom, where his indictment is read out. He is charged with six crimes: three counts of high treason as an alien, and the three identical charges as a citizen. The defence lawyers argue the unfairness of this, but the judge shuts them down. Louis is to stand trial both as a foreigner and as a subject of the Queen. The defence then questions the jurisdiction, hoping to move the trial closer to Louis's home turf. Again, the judge shuts them down. Finally, the lawyers ask for the trial to be delayed by a month, so that they can prepare and, just as importantly, bring two doctors from asylums where Louis was kept back east. But the defence's biggest surprise of the day is to request that Gabriel Dumont himself be allowed to testify, to tell the court that it was the Exovedate, not Riel, who voted to wage war against Canada and Gabriel, not Louis, who carried out military operations. The lawyers want a guarantee of immunity for Gabriel if he is to come back to Canada. And for a third time in a day, the judge refuses them. They will have one week only to prepare for what the Crown calls the most serious trial ever to be held in Canada.

Move ahead a week: the trial of Louis Riel for high treason opens on the morning of July 28, 1885. Six male jury members are seated. The Crown then outlines its evidence against Louis, including his breaking with the priests of Saskatchewan and his offer to return to Montana if he was given a large sum of money from the federal government. The Crown then declares, "I think you will be satisfied before this case is over that it is not a matter brought about by any wrongs so much as a matter brought about by the personal ambition and vanity of the man on trial."

Not a matter brought about by any wrongs? Louis thinks. The Métis have been wronged countless times by the government and by greedy land-grabbers. It is completely based on wrongs! As for personal ambition and vanity, Louis knows that his ambition is for his people and that God disdains vanity. The Crown doesn't know him at all. Louis looks around this tiny courtroom, no more than fifty feet by twenty and filled with reporters and the fancily dressed wives of the Crown prosecutors and General Middleton and the judge. No, these people don't know him at all, and they are a world away from the hardscrabble life of the children of the prairies. His stomach must sink at this thought. He will not be given a fair trial. It is impossible.

The Crown's first witness is John Willoughby, a Saskatoon doctor who'd purportedly talked to Riel at the outset of the rebellion. When it comes time for the defence to cross-examine him, Louis listens as his lawyers question Willoughby about what had been discussed. Mainly, it seems they'd talked about Louis's idea to divide up the vast lands of the North-West, not just among the Métis but among different groups of immigrants who were arriving weekly to settle and farm. The defence makes it sound as if Louis's idea that there is enough land for everyone isn't a sane one. When one of Louis's lawyers asks Willoughby if this seemed like a very rational proposition, the witness replies quickly, "It did not." But it is! What exactly is the defence up to? They've kept their strategy quiet. Louis suddenly feels worried.

Witnesses for the Crown continue to line up through the rest of the day, each piling on more and more damaging evidence. A man who was a prisoner of Riel's testifies that he witnessed the prophet commanding armed Métis and remembers hearing Louis brag about ordering his men to open fire at Duck Lake, as well as talking of needing another victory. Other witnesses acknowledge that Louis was the brain behind the whole operation. Again and again in cross-examination, Louis watches in growing horror as his lawyers push the witnesses to discuss what will surely be viewed as his oddities, including frequent mood swings and eating cooked blood for his health. While the Crown tries to make Louis appear cold and calculating, his own lawyers are clearly building the argument that Louis is sick mentally. He now sees where this is leading: they will argue that he is insane, and therefore not guilty as charged. But if they are successful in arguing this, then the rest of Canada and the world may think that the Métis cause is just as insane. Louis ponders this as the day wears on, realizing with each attack against his sanity that he cannot allow this to happen, for it will destroy his people, and his dream.

On the second day of the trial, the Crown continues to argue that Louis acted in a cold and calculating manner, actively and sanely fomenting rebellion among a group of poor half-breeds, manipulating them with his devilish ideas. George Kerr, the store owner in Batoche, takes the stand and recounts the meetings Louis held in the lead-up to the rebellion. The brother of Louis's former secretary, Honoré Jaxon (previously known as Will Jackson), speaks of how Louis was able to control the poor bastard, who himself is mentally unstable. Louis watches and listens carefully as first General Middleton, then Captain Young (who accompanied Louis from Batoche to his trial), speak to his intelligence and knowledge of world affairs. Louis watches with deep sadness when his own cousin, Charles Nolin, takes the stand to speak against him. Charles, who supported a Métis uprising in the beginning, has turned against his own blood and people, supplying key knowledge of the intricacies of the rebellion. This is not the first time that Charles has been a Judas. Back in 1870 after Red River, he'd done the same thing, crossing his own cousin for political gain. But Louis, rather than feeling anger, feels only sadness for the spineless man.

Louis does get angry, though, when his defence team begins questioning cousin Charles about Louis's sanity. Charles admits that Louis believes he can prophesy the future based on how his body's organs react to his commands, and that he becomes uncontrollably excited and angry whenever he hears the word "police." This questioning must stop! Louis is not insane! He must set things straight. Louis stands up and begins speaking to the judge. "If there is any way, by legal procedure, that I should be allowed to say a word, I wish you would allow me before this witness leaves the box."

The judge responds by telling Louis that he must bring this up with his own counsel through the proper channels, but Louis continues. "Do you allow me to speak? I have some observation to make before the court."

Louis's lawyers are mortified. Fitzpatrick tells him that this is not the proper time. Pointing to Louis, he says, "He must not be allowed to interfere," and the judge points out that Louis has the right to counsel but also the right to defend himself.

Filled with emotion, Louis speaks again. "Your Honour, this case comes to be extraordinary, and while the Crown, with the great talents they have at their service, are trying to show I am guilty—of course it is their duty—my counsellors are trying—my good friends and lawyers who have been sent here by friends whom I respect—are trying to show that I am insane."

Once again the judge orders Louis to be quiet and tells him that he must put his questions through his counsel. Fitzpatrick, sensing he's losing control not just of the case but of his client, again asks the judge to forbid Louis from interrupting.

Richardson, suddenly realizing that Louis hasn't been informed of their plans, addresses Louis's lawyers. "I don't like to dictate to you, but it strikes me that now an opportunity should be taken of ascertaining whether there is really anything that has not been put to this witness that ought to have been put."

Angry now, Fitzpatrick quickly answers that he has the discretion to make his case. A quietly delighted Crown prosecutor steps in to say that he'd be happy for Louis himself to ask questions if this is what Louis desires.

Judge Richardson asks Louis the question that hovers in the courtroom: "Prisoner, are you defended by counsel?" Louis doesn't answer, just stares down at his notes in front of him. Again the judge asks, then again and finally again, "Prisoner, are you defended by counsel?"

Finally, Louis gives his answer:

> I will, if you please, say this. My counsel come from Quebec, from a far province. They have to put questions to men with whom they are not acquainted, on circumstances which they don't know; and although I am willing to give them all the information that I can, they cannot follow the thread of all the questions that should be put to the witnesses. They lose more than three quarters of the good opportunities. Not because they are not able! They are learned, they are talented; but the circumstances are such that they cannot put all

the questions. If I would be allowed—as it was suggested, this case is extraordinary!

Again, Judge Richardson tells Louis that he will have the opportunity to speak at the appointed time.

"I cannot all," Louis says, "I cannot all. I have too much to say. There is too much to say."

After a few minutes' recess for the defence to pull itself together, Louis makes the decision to keep his counsel. What other choice does he have? His English isn't good enough to defend himself, and there is so much to say, so much to explain, that it would take him months of preparation. It is better to keep this counsel than to be left alone. Once more though, against the wishes of the court and his defence, Louis feels the urge to explain himself. "I cannot abandon my dignity! Here I have to defend myself against the accusation of high treason, or I have to consent to the animal life of an asylum. I don't care much about animal life if I am not allowed to carry with it the moral existence of an intellectual being."

Angrily, the judge raises his voice. "Now, stop!"

"Yes, Your Honour," Louis whispers.

For the rest of the day the Crown piles on the damaging evidence: a letter Louis wrote to Poundmaker, begging him to join the rebellion; witnesses who recall seeing Louis, crucifix in hand, exhorting the half-breeds to carry on the killing of policemen. By the end of the second day when the Crown rests its case, Louis has been painted as a calculating instigator and mastermind.

Now it's the defence's turn. On the morning of July 30, the defence opens by calling on Father Alexis André, the priest who, above all, considers Louis a heretic and a madman. Expecting to hear the priest denigrate him, Louis is instead surprised to hear André explain how for years, petition after petition, the Métis begged the federal government to treat them with justice and fairness, to settle their title for the land upon which they'd lived and settled, and how year after year, the government ignored the half-breeds.

The Crown angrily interjects that the defence is playing unfairly by having André describe why the rebellion might have been justified, when their true aim is to prove that Louis is insane. The two defences are inconsistent, the Crown argues, and this argument rages through the length of the priest's testimony. By the end of it, Louis is excited to see that André has made it clear that the government is also to blame for the violence that erupted. But just as quickly, Louis is dismayed once more when the priest speaks to

Louis's mental state, calling him a "fool," "not in control of himself," and "not responsible."

Other witnesses contend that Louis is a madman. A member of his own Exovedate, Philippe Garnot, admits, "I thought the man was crazy," especially when it came to his rather bizarre prayers. Father Fourmond, who follows, talks more about Louis's religious oddities and his grave mood swings. But when they are cross-examined, all three men only strengthen the Crown's case by admitting that Louis was clearly the leader of the Métis.

The fourth witness, Doctor François-Elzéar Roy, a part-owner of the asylum in Quebec City where Louis spent nineteen months, testifies that he suffers from what the doctor labels megalomania. Roy's cross-examination becomes the battle of the day. For more than an hour he fences with the Crown about the nature of insanity. The Crown insults the doctor by claiming his asylum is nothing more than a boarding house, but Roy, without benefit of his files or records of Louis's stay, argues lucidly in English and then in French. By all accounts, he bests the Crown at its own game and offers a glimmer of hope to the defence.

The next witness for the defence is Doctor Daniel Clark, another psychiatrist, this one from Toronto. He has arrived at the last minute as a substitute for a doctor who treated

Louis but wasn't able to come. Doctor Clark spoke with Louis three times over the course of two days, and his limited knowledge of the half-breed and his temperament does little good for anyone.

And with these five men, and in less than one full day, the defence rests its case. The Crown calls its rebuttal witnesses and steadily builds its case through the rest of the third day and into the fourth. A doctor who runs an asylum in Hamilton, Ontario, argues that Louis is indeed sane, as do Captain Young and General Middleton, who speak to Louis's intelligence. A minister and two Mounties who spent time with Louis also agree about his sanity.

Day four ends with Fitzpatrick giving a two-hour address that spills over into the fifth day. The crux of his argument is what Louis and Gabriel and the others had been saying all along: that the Government of Canada "had wholly failed in its duty toward these North-West Territories." He also maintains his stand that Louis is not sane, ending his talk by pleading to the six-man jury, "I know that you shall not weave the cord that shall hang him and hang him high in the face of all the world, a poor confirmed lunatic—a victim, gentlemen, of oppression or the victim of fanaticism." With that, he rests his case.

Judge Richardson now turns to Louis, and the moment Louis has been both looking forward to and dreading arrives. Some say Louis's speech is brilliant, others that it is rambling and confused. The fact is that Louis decides to speak in English for fear of not being able to control any translation. Although he can speak English, it isn't his strong suit. But what other choice does he have?

"Your Honours," Louis begins, "gentlemen of the jury":

It would be easy for me today to play insanity, because the circumstances are such as to excite any man, and under the natural excitement of what is taking place today (I cannot speak English very well, but am trying to do so, because most of those here speak English), under the excitement which my trial causes me would justify me not to appear as usual, but with my mind out of its ordinary condition. I hope with the help of God I will maintain calmness and decorum as suits this honourable court, this honourable jury.

Louis looks to all the strangers staring at him. There is so much he needs to explain to them. But how? Where to begin? He remembers, right then, what is most important.

Begging the audience not to think of him as insane, Louis then recites a prayer, asking God to bless all of those present.

And then Louis begins to try to explain himself, to explain his actions, to explain the plight of his beloved people:

> When I came into the North-West in July, the first of July 1884, I found the Indians suffering. I found the half-breeds eating the rotten pork of the Hudson Bay Company and getting sick and weak every day. Although a half-breed, and having no pretension to help the whites, I also paid attention to them. I saw they were deprived of responsible government, I saw that they were deprived of their public liberties. I remembered that half-breed meant white and Indian, and while I paid attention to the suffering Indians and the half-breeds I remembered that the greatest part of my heart and blood was white, and I have directed my attention to help the Indians, to help the half-breeds and to help the whites to the best of my ability. We have made petitions, I have made petitions with others to the Canadian Government asking to relieve the condition of this country. We have taken time; we have tried to unite all classes, even if I may speak,

all parties. Those who have been in close communication with me know I have suffered, that I have waited for months to bring some of the people of the Saskatchewan to an understanding of certain important points in our petition to the Canadian Government and I have done my duty. I believe I have done my duty.

The words come to Louis, and he is excited about this. He pushes on, tries to explain the complexities, defending himself against the charges the Crown has made that he is vain, that he works to enrich himself. He tries to explain that his lawyers could not ask the right questions of the witnesses because they don't fully understand the situation, but Louis's English words begin to fail him. He must pull it together; he must find the thread again.

"It is true, gentlemen, I believed for years I had a mission, and when I speak of a mission you will understand me not as trying to play the role of insane before the grand jury so as to have a verdict of acquittal upon that ground. I believe that I have a mission, I believe I had a mission at this very time." Yes, this is it. Louis explains his mission in the past, how he helped Manitoba and how he was punished by the government for doing so. But then Bishop Bourget was able to recognize that Louis had a mission to fulfill, and others did as well. Louis explains that other holy men have blessed him too. But he begins to get lost in the details, needs once again to find that thread.

> Today when I saw the glorious General Middleton
> bearing testimony that he thought I was not
> insane, and when Captain Young proved that I am
> not insane, I felt that God was blessing me, and
> blotting away from my name the blot resting upon
> my reputation on account of having been in the
> lunatic asylum of my good friend Dr. Roy. I have
> been in an asylum, but I thank the lawyers for the
> Crown who destroyed the testimony of my good
> friend Dr. Roy, because I have always believed that
> I was put in the asylum without reason.

Yes, defend yourself, Louis. Explain to them all that you are not mad. But then Louis again becomes lost in the English words when he begins speaking of his Judas cousin Charles Nolin, and so he turns back to the agitation that he helped begin and his respect for the police. But it's too easy to become lost in the blame, to blame the priests who are wrong, who are instruments of God but who have been broken. Louis struggles to find the right words again. The people in the courtroom stare at him; some fidget, others yawn in the midday heat. He must find the thread again. The people here must understand!

Louis explains what he means when he says Rome has fallen, that the plagues of the Old World don't need to continue in the New. But then the hurt of what his cousin Nolin said about Louis claiming he can predict the future by the noise of his bowels leads him astray again. Find the thread! Find the thread! Louis tries to defend his thinking that the North-West should be divided into sevenths and given to the immigrants from Europe alongside the Métis and Indians. And, despite what the jury might think, Louis can't help informing them one more time, "I am no more than you are, I am simply one of the flock, equal to the rest. If it is any satisfaction to the doctors to know what kind of insanity I have, if they are going to call my pretensions insanity, I say humbly, through the grace of God, I believe I am the prophet of the New World."

There, Louis has said it, and he thinks he's said it in such a way that the jury and the judge and the people in fine clothes who listen to him won't think he's bragging. His own people declared Louis a prophet, not Louis. He feels steady with his words once more. Louis thinks he has found a way to finish this, to come to the sane conclusion of it all:

If you take the plea of the defence that I am not responsible for my acts, acquit me completely since I have been quarrelling with an insane and irresponsible Government. If you pronounce in favour of the Crown, which contends that I am responsible, acquit me all the same. You are perfectly justified in declaring that having my reason and sound mind, I have acted reasonably and in self-defence, while the Government, my accuser, being irresponsible, and consequently insane, cannot but have acted wrong, and if high treason there is it must be on its side and not on my part.

Judge Richardson asks Louis if he is done. Louis thinks about this for a moment. Is he? Is he done? So much to say. So little time. They all must understand him. "Not yet," Louis says, "if you have the kindness to permit me your attention for a while." Louis explains that despite what others see as his vanity, he has never been particular about his clothing. But more than that, others, including the priests, have often had to feed his family. He explains that he is simply a guest of this country, a guest who works tirelessly for the betterment of his people. But he has lost the thread again. He's now begging for the mercy of the court, for its understanding. Rather than ending on a powerful note, the English words escape Louis, and his speech peters out trying to explain this. "I put my speech under the protection of my God, my Saviour, He is the only one who can make it effective. It is possible it should become effective, as it is proposed to good men, to good people, and to good ladies also." This is not how he wished to end it, but this is how it ends.

The next morning, the final morning of the trial, Judge Richardson has strong words for the jury before they retire to decide Louis's fate. He shoots down any possible defence that Louis is an American citizen and can't be tried as a Canadian. He also tells the jury in no uncertain terms that their responsibility is two-pronged: first, is Louis guilty of treason? And second, if he is guilty, can he be held responsible mentally? But Richardson doesn't stop there. In fact, he leads the jury to what its answer should be. "Not only must you think of the man in the dock," Richardson says, "but you must think of society at large. You are not called upon to think of the Government at Ottawa simply as a Government, you have to think of the homes and of the people who live in this country, you have to ask yourselves: Can such things be permitted?" If ever a command by a judge on how he expects a jury to respond has been uttered, Louis has just heard it.

At 2 P.M. on August 1, 1885, the six men leave to decide whether Louis Riel will live or not. The talking is done. The arguing is over. Louis, alone in the crush of people who chatter and sweat and laugh in their fine clothing, kneels down in the prisoner box and begins to pray. He speaks the words out loud, begs God for forgiveness and for enlightenment, unaware that he makes the white people who have now stopped chattering and begun staring at him uncomfortable with this display. Louis thinks of the small statue of Saint Joseph back in his cell, the one he holds and prays feverishly to every day. Not long ago he dropped it and to his horror, the head snapped off when it hit the hard ground. It's clear to Louis what his own fate will be.

Less than an hour and a half later, at 3:20 P.M., the jury returns. None of them make eye contact with Louis. The clerk asks him to rise. He does. "Gentlemen," the clerk says, "are you agreed upon the verdict?"

The foreman stands. "We find the defendant guilty," he says, causing Louis to sway. The clerk asks all of the jury if this is their decision. They nod and mumble yes. But then the foreman speaks up. "Your Honour," he says. "I have been asked by my brother jurors to recommend the prisoner to the mercy of the Crown." Judge Richardson agrees to let this be known to the proper authorities. He then looks to Louis one more time, asks with a tinge of exhaustion in his voice if he has anything else to say.

Louis stands a final time. He expresses his relief that he isn't judged an insane man and that hopefully, in this way, his mission can still be fulfilled. He thanks the jurors for recommending clemency and adds that he hopes the verdict just handed down might prove once and for all that he really is a prophet, just as his Biblical namesake was.

"I have been hunted like an elk for fifteen years," Louis says to the court. "David had been [hunted for] seventeen [years]: I think I will have to be about two years still. But I hope it will come sooner." He again apologizes for his poor English. He speaks of how he helped Manitoba come into existence but once more loses the thread and finds himself droning on about the seven nationalities settling the North-West and of the Americans coming to help his cause and then of his dear friend Gabriel who works this very moment to free him. He feels weak and stops speaking for a minute. Where is the thread?

Judge Richardson asks if Louis is done. No, Louis and his work will never be done. He explains that the Manitoba Act of 1870 has not been fulfilled, that he has never received compensation for his hard work. Louis says he believes that a special commission should be convened to hear his case.

This can't possibly be all there is to it, to his work, to his life! For the first time, for the last time, Louis finds the thread, wraps it around his hands so tightly that he will never lose it again. He recognizes this very moment that he is on trial for being Métis, that he is on trial for daring to have decided that white men, especially those dogs like Thomas Scott, could indeed be forced to answer to the Métis people. Louis is on trial for being a half-breed, a half-breed who refuses to bow down to the people in front of him. He is being judged for his inability to bow down.

Judge Richardson is cold in his answer. He wishes, Louis realizes, to crush him and crush his people, once and for all. "For what you did the remarks you have made form no excuse whatsoever. For what you have done the law requires you to answer." The judge goes on, explaining to Louis that he should not expect the hand of clemency, that Louis will now be taken back to his cell where he will be kept until September 18, where he will be "taken to the place appointed for your execution, and there be hanged by the neck till you are dead. And may God have mercy on your soul."

CHAPTER THIRTEEN

Hunting

As the summer of 1885 blossoms, more Métis from Saskatchewan join Gabriel in Montana. Gabriel listens to them chatter like evening birds about invading the North-West, but he's given up on the plan. He will travel to Regina and serve as a witness for Louis. This is the most realistic course. But when he hears word that he won't be offered amnesty and then, not long after this, that his friend has been handed the death penalty, Gabriel resurrects his plan to rescue Louis from his jail cell. He rides restlessly through the communities of Montana, drumming up support and even organizing a route from Saskatchewan into the U.S. with a number of safe houses where he and Louis can rest briefly, be fed, and change horses.

For reasons only Gabriel knows, though, the plan is never enacted. Part of it, surely, is that whatever ragged force he can drum up will be no challenge for the hundreds of Mounties currently guarding Louis. But Gabriel's never been afraid of a fight before. It isn't simply that he's outnumbered.

He looks around him at the defeated Métis, like his friend Michel Dumas, who has turned to drinking heavily and is making a fool of himself. Gabriel finds out that he too is being watched closely by spies of the Canadian government, some of them Métis who have been tempted by a few dollars of dirty money. His wife has just joined him here in Montana and frets when Gabriel collapses and blacks out from the head wound that still haunts him. The Métis, he sadly realizes, are in no shape to put up another fight against the Canadians. Gabriel will just lead more of them to slaughter. He instead prays to the Virgin Mary that his friend Louis will be saved from the gallows with a pardon from John A. It's all, depressingly, out of Gabriel's hands now.

He begins to believe the Virgin is listening to him when friends read him stories in papers from all over the world condemning Louis's execution. The government of France speaks out strongly against such a barbaric act as hanging a man who never fired a shot in anger and who is a political prisoner, not a criminal one. England and the United States follow suit, editorials from papers across both countries urging the government to reconsider. Politicians from around the world write letters to the Canadian government condemning the planned execution. Gabriel smiles the day in September that he hears Louis's execution has been post-poned. Surely John A. will bow to international pressure.

But the Ontario papers rage with anger and scream for Louis's head. And, as if to let the Orangemen know exactly where he stands and what will indeed happen to Mr. Riel, John A. makes his infamous remark to critics of his decision to kill Louis: "He shall hang, though every dog in Quebec bark in his favour!"

As if in foreshadowing, Wandering Spirit and ten other Indians are hanged for their involvement in the uprising, eight of them together from the same scaffold in a ghastly scene of mass execution as witnesses cheer. Gabriel takes some solace, though, when he hears that a number of his men from the Exovedate who had been charged with felony-treason have been handed between one and seven years in prison instead of the noose. Big Bear, who has finally surren-dered after a lengthy running battle with the Canadians, is sentenced, along with Poundmaker, to three years. They are both released early, in 1887, and both die shortly thereafter, their spirits and their people crushed by the continued onslaught of the settling of the Dominion.

What Gabriel can't know is that John A. has once again called a secret enquiry to weigh the current state of Louis Riel's mind. John A., it appears, wants to cover his own political assets by having a group of doctors tell him what he wants to hear: that Louis Riel is indeed sane and fit to be hanged by the neck until dead. When one doctor argues that Louis is in fact insane, his report is slashed from the enquiry. The heavily censored document finally gives John A. the green light. He is not putting to death a madman. Despite numerous appeals, Louis's execution is scheduled for November 16, 1885. The Canadian government has pushed hard to get this done as expediently as possible, so that they might leave this most distasteful mess behind and get on with completing the railway and furthering the business of the Dominion.

Gabriel, like his dear friend and leader Louis, hopes against hope that some justice will eventually visit the Métis and that Louis will be spared the gallows. They both hope until the eve of November 16, right up until it becomes clear that all appeals have failed and the scaffold has been built beside Louis's cell. Friends tell Gabriel about the last hours of Louis's life, of how he never wavers, never cries out or begs for mercy, never shows weakness. Instead, Louis stays up the night before his execution with Father André; by a strange twist, the man who was once Louis's nemesis has now become his confessor and his spiritual counsellor.

In the last months of Louis's captivity, Father André had made sure to make himself available for confession and for communion, and he's worked diligently to convince Louis that what he did was wrong and a sin in God's eyes. Louis, beaten down now by a system bent on his destruction, must get a strong whiff of his own mortality as the hammers echo out the construction of his gallows right next to his window. On this last night of his life, he kneels for hours with his confessor, prays to the Lord for his forgiveness and for the protection of his friends and family and his Métis people. Louis writes letters to his wife and to his mother and to his children, is focused and appears as far away from insanity as any man can be. Louis's mission now is to face his own death with the calm and the pride of the Métis. He is indeed focused, has been since that last day of his trial when he realized so absolutely that this was not just about him, but about his people, a people too free to surrender.

At 5 A.M., Father André administers Louis's last mass and communion. Louis asks permission to bathe, and then frets after as he dresses that the clothes in which he is to die—a white shirt, a black jacket, brown coarse trousers, and a pair of well-made and prettily beaded moccasins—are too shabby. The guardroom in which he is kept has a second floor and a blacksmith cuts away the iron bars on the window from which Louis will emerge onto the scaffolding. The precautions taken to prevent Gabriel from sweeping in and rescuing Louis are quite extraordinary. A high fence has been built around the gallows, which angers locals and travellers alike, who now won't be able to witness the violent death of this man. And every Mountie in Regina and beyond stands guard with a loaded weapon.

At 8:15 A.M., as Louis and Father André are talking quietly, the deputy in charge appears at Louis's cell door. "You want me?" Louis asks him. "I am ready." With that, Louis stands and, policemen on either side, walks up the steps slowly but steadily to the second floor and waits in front of the barless window, a small crucifix in his hand. Father André follows, shaking so much that he cannot make it up the stairs without the help of officials and another priest. One last time, Father André and Louis kneel, and Louis whispers that he forgives his enemies, repents his sins, and offers his life as a sacrifice to God. When his friends tell Gabriel this last part, he understands how it is that Louis went so bravely. He has always acted best and strongest when he sacrificed for the people, and especially for God.

Before they stand, Father André requests that Louis keep his promise to refrain from speaking any last words in public when asked if he wishes to do so. He doesn't want Louis undoing in the last minutes what André has worked so hard these last months to accomplish: the return of his ward to the fold. Louis promises he won't. Kneeling now in the shadow of the gallows, Louis has no more speeches in him. With that, they stand. The police take Louis's hands, bend his head forward, and help him step out the window and onto the scaffold.

The morning is bright and cold. Despite this, Louis sweats. He can feel the beads of it on his face. A cold sweat. A night sweat like one that comes with bad dreams. As Father André walks with him to where the rope awaits, the priest stumbles, and Louis whispers for him to have courage. By the gallows now, a rope is placed loosely about Louis's neck. The deputy asks if there are any last words. Louis can hear Father André crying, his head turned away. "Shall I say something?" Louis asks, concerned now for the priest's weakness. Maybe there is something still to be said.

"No," the priest chokes.

Louis requests time to pray some more. He is given two minutes. The other priest accompanying the party, this one sent by sympathizers from Toronto, suggests that Louis recite the Lord's Prayer. The priest then leans to the deputy and tells him to command the hangman to pull the lever when Louis reaches the line "… deliver us from evil." The deputy nods. It isn't so much an act of cruelty as one of mercy. Louis won't suspect it at that moment.

Gabriel must shake with anger when he is told of this next part, the last cruel twist of injustice: the hangman approaches Louis, places a white cotton hood over his head, tucks it beneath the rope before roughly tightening the cord about his neck, then spits in Louis's ear, "Louis Riel, do you know me? You cannot escape from me today!" As it turns out, a man who bears a personal grudge against Louis has been allowed to act as his executioner, something even the most barbaric of societies frown upon. The executioner claims to have been taken prisoner by Riel's men in the Red River Resistance back in 1870, and he further claims to have been a friend of the rabid dog Thomas Scott. The executioner has waited fifteen years for the chance to whisper this to Louis. His ugly words mar an otherwise respectful day.

Ironically, the last words, the last prayer, of Louis's life are spoken in English. As the Toronto priest has requested, while the last line of the Lord's Prayer is being recited, the trap door springs open and Louis, not yet quite ready, falls nine feet before his body jerks to a stop and then begins to convulse. Over the course of two minutes the convulsions continue, slowing eventually to twitches and then, finally, to stillness. Father André, reporting it all to his superiors, writes, "Riel died a saint."

SOMETHING BREAKS IN GABRIEL on November 16, 1885. Something breaks in all of the Métis. Louis's wife, Marguerite, dies of what the doctor labels tuberculosis only six months later, in May of 1886. She'd lost their third child to miscarriage just a month before Louis was executed and had stopped caring about life completely when her husband was taken away for good. Louis's only daughter, Angelique, dies of diphtheria shortly before her fourteenth birthday, and his only son, Jean, dies in 1908 when his buggy overturns. There will be no direct descendants for Louis David Riel.

Tragedy visits Gabriel, too, not long after Louis's death. His beloved wife, Madeleine, passes away in 1886, just a few weeks after Louis's wife. Doctors claim consumption is the culprit. Childless, Gabriel is distraught. But he's also the last of the leaders of the buffalo hunt and knows that he sets an example for all of his people. He makes a deal with himself to carry on.

Now that Gabriel is a full-fledged fugitive of Canadian law as well as a bona fide hero of the plains, it makes great sense to Buffalo Bill Cody to include him in his famous "Wild West" show. Cody was so intrigued that he sent

JOSEPH BOYDEN

emissaries shortly after Gabriel arrived in Montana following the failure at Batoche, but Gabriel summarily turned
them down. He had Louis to try to save. But now Gabriel
has very little to hold him in one place, and the money is
tempting. Gabriel has always lived by the rhythms of the
hunt, eating well when it was good, going lean when it
wasn't. But the hunting here in Montana cannot sustain a
man. And besides, joining the show will allow Gabriel to see
places he's never imagined.

In June of 1886, just over a year after he'd fled his beloved
home, Gabriel takes a train to New York and marks an X on
the contract offered to him by Buffalo Bill. Gabriel's act
shows off his riding skills and especially his marksmanship.
He shares the stage with Annie Oakley, shooting glass balls
tossed up in the air as he charges full stride on horseback.
He, along with the others, draws full crowds. He's a real live
outlaw, and he's magic with his most prized possession, his
rifle *le petit*. But Gabriel doesn't speak English, doesn't feel in
the least bit at home as he travels the northeast coast of the
United States, except for the times he shares meals with the
Sioux warriors who have also joined the circus.

And then word comes in July of 1886 that Gabriel, along
with all the other Métis who fled, is being offered amnesty by
the Canadian government, something it hadn't dared to do

174

just one year before when Gabriel had hoped to defend his friend in court. Suddenly, Gabriel's cachet as an outlaw is tarnished. He is also homesick for the west, so he and Buffalo Bill agree that he will be free after he completes his original three-month contract. The two men also agree that Gabriel is at liberty to make special appearances whenever he likes, which Gabriel does, periodically, over the next number of years.

But now what to do? Gabriel has no trust for the words and promises of John A. and the others. This might all be a trick. Instead of rushing back home, he agrees to some speaking engagements for expatriate and well-to-do French Canadians living in the American northeast. For the next year, Gabriel accepts some of these invitations grudgingly. Louis was the orator, after all. Gabriel was simply the actor. In his simple and straightforward language, he hits this lecture circuit, a hero and an oddity to these people who are only partially his. He is given silver medals and a gold watch and money to live on, but this isn't a natural act for Gabriel, this standing in front of an audience as he sweats in his suit, trying to explain his love for his land, how he misses his people, so many of them scattered to the wind.

IT'S VERY EASY to become lost in such circumstances, Gabriel realizes, and he begins to wander, trying to figure out what to do in the years after Louis's death. Some even claim that he travels as far as France, searching for what has been taken from him. He does certainly travel back and forth between Montana and New York. Even though he now knows he really is allowed to return home, he doesn't. His wife is dead, his parents are dead, so many of his brothers are dead. Louis is gone forever, and so is Gabriel's old way of life. Like his dear friend before him, he has been cast out into the wilderness. But this wilderness, part concrete and massive buildings in the east, part poverty and survival hunting in the west, is not the place Gabriel ever envisioned his life would lead him.

While the fame of being himself, the leader of the North-West Rebellion, is somewhat enticing, it's always the Métis, his people, that keep Gabriel grounded. They are suffering miserably now that they have been beaten down. Gabriel finds a focus in the late 1880s, once again writing petitions with the help of his old friend, Maxime Lépine, urging the people of Quebec to not forget their western cousins, explaining that the Métis still deserve land scrip, and that Gabriel and others should be compensated for the loss of their properties.

Gabriel returns home to Canada in the spring of 1888, heading to Montreal with plans of lecturing and, in his own small way, picking up where Louis left off. He's been told by people who claim to have his best interests in mind that it's time to dictate his autobiography, but both plans are stymied by the powerful priests of Quebec, who fear he will agitate too much once more. Certain Quebec politicians see a wonderful tool in Gabriel if only they can get him to become a better public speaker. Quebec nationalism is rising, and Québécois politicians hope Gabriel can help them in their fight for stronger provincial powers. But Gabriel knows in his heart that, for all his desire, he will never be the speaker Louis was. In his speeches thus far, the only way Gabriel resembles Louis is that he opposes the priests who do more harm than good for his people, but in Quebec, loyalty to the Catholic Church is one rule that must not be broken.

Finally, in 1890, five full years after the fighting at Batoche and not long after Gabriel dictates his memoirs about that event, he returns home to Saskatchewan. He finds things so painfully changed—squatters on the land, his friends and family scattered, his Indian friends on their reserves in such dire poverty—that he realizes he doesn't want to stay. He travels back to the U.S. once more, this time to Dakota and Métis hunting camps that promise him at least a semblance of his old life.

The last publicized event in Gabriel's life is a violent episode, and it occurs, ironically, while he's surrounded by friends. One night in 1891, as he sleeps in his tent in a Dakota hunting camp, Gabriel is attacked by an assassin wielding a knife. The man stabs Gabriel in the head and then in the body. Gabriel, strong as a buffalo—and as thick-headed as one, too, he later jokes—grabs the man's knife with his hand, the blade lacerating his palm deeply, and in this way wrenches it away before wrestling the man into submission. Gabriel's shouts bring the rest of the camp running, and after trying to surmise who the man is and especially who sent him, Gabriel magnanimously lets him go, possibly as a warning to the man's bosses that they cannot kill Gabriel. He believes until the day he dies, fifteen years later, that the assassin was sent by the Canadian government.

After another stint trying to raise money in Quebec for impoverished Métis out west, Gabriel returns home for the final time in 1893. He's fifty-six years old now and ready for the last battle of his life. He first settled his land at Gabriel's Crossing in 1872, and still, twenty-one years on and despite all that's happened, the government has ignored his repeated requests for official ownership. It won't be for another nine years—in a new century, in the year 1902—that the government finally agrees to give him title to it. Thirty years he's struggled to be recognized as the one who lives on this land honestly, and thirty years later he finally wins what, in the scheme of things, is a small but decisive victory.

These last years of his life, as an old century becomes a new one, Gabriel turns inward and to the land, as always, hunting, trapping, and fishing it for his survival. Rather than rebuilding at Gabriel's Crossing, he lives on his relatives' land in a small log cabin. Perhaps there are too many painful memories at the Crossing on the South Saskatchewan, or perhaps now that he finally has title to the land, the Sarcee in him tells him that to think one can actually own the earth is the white man's folly. Perhaps it's Gabriel's quiet way of telling John A. and the rest that they will never control him. Perhaps it's all these things and more.

After returning from a hunting trip in mid-May of 1906, sixty-nine-year-old Gabriel complains of pain in his chest and arms. The pain goes away in a day or two, and Gabriel, thinking it tired muscles, visits an old friend on May 19. As is the custom, he's offered some food, and after a couple of bites, Gabriel stands up and walks a few steps before collapsing. He's dead before he hits the floor.

Only a few tiny local papers report the death of the man who, twenty years before, held the fear and grudging respect of a nation. But on the day Gabriel is buried in the tiny cemetery on the rise at Batoche, nestled in along with his comrades from that long-ago fighting, Métis in their sashes begin to arrive, Cree from Beardy's and One Arrow's reserves, too. They come streaming in on horse and by foot, in Red River cart or by canoe, to celebrate the life of the last of the leaders of the buffalo hunt. Some of the wiser ones burn sweetgrass and sage and tobacco, do it knowing that each morning, as the sun begins to rise, the spirit of Gabriel will rise with it. He is a real hunter, a real leader, after all, and so he will always have no choice but to rise with the sun.

I stand with my hands up on the chain-link fence, staring at the place, a stone's throw away, where Louis Riel was hanged. There's no statue, no marker, no way you'd ever know that this is the spot without some pretty serious research and a touch of the detective in you. I'm on the edge of a property called the "Depot," in Regina, Saskatchewan. It's the home and training grounds of our country's RCMP. I'd wanted to stand in that place where Louis hovered above the ground in the last instant of his life, but no one with the proper authority is available today to accompany me. And so I'm here, with my hands up on the fence, a Métis outsider staring in at the old chapel that was once the guardhouse that held Louis.

Maybe it's a little morbid, but I can picture Louis stepping out of the second-storey window of this chapel that was once the guardhouse and onto the scaffolding of the long-gone gallows, bookended by policemen and followed by a crying Father André with his long white beard and black robes. I can picture Louis with the rope around his neck staring ahead and mumbling prayers under his breath, questioning for a moment how he ended up here in this place on this day, the last one of his life. Does he regret his actions as he stands on the scaffold?

THE YEAR BEFORE MY VISIT to Regina I fly to Saskatoon, rent a car at the small airport, and begin to drive. It's a gorgeous summer day, the prairie fields exploding with wildflowers. I'm surprised as I drive north how these prairies aren't flat at all but undulate like waves on a great ocean. I try to picture Gabriel riding through this same country, hunting buffalo as a younger man or, as he hits middle age, evading the military as he rides away from Batoche to a different kind of captivity from Louis's, this one in the States.

I turn east off the main highway onto a secondary one and then onto an even smaller road. Following this, I'm surprised to feel my heart rate quicken as I close in on my first destination. As the wide river comes in sight, sparkling in the brilliant sunshine, I smile to myself, understanding now in this very moment why a people would be willing to fight and die for such a place. It's beautiful, the poplar leaves along the river shimmering in the breeze, the South Saskatchewan curving like a smile. I drive slowly over the steel bridge that is Gabriel's Crossing, taking it all in: the shining water, the thick growth of trees along the bank, the fertile ground sloping up and stretching out for miles. The only structure around, a well-kept house with a large teepee in the backyard, piques my interest. I won't bother the owner today. Instead, I continue my exploration.

I take my time, travelling unimpeded through the square miles surrounding Batoche, surveying a couple of the original rifle pits protecting the village, spending a few hours at the annual Back to Batoche Festival, driving out to Fish Creek and seeing first-hand the place where Gabriel not only held off Middleton and his army but beat them soundly when they dared encroach too close to his home. It's almost as if I wander through a dream, traversing this country that was Gabriel Dumont's. Something tells me he never did regret his actions. And I can see now, absorbing the majesty of this land, that neither did Louis.

The fenced-in Depot in Regina and the wide-open country surrounding Batoche could not be more different. They represent the two worlds of the Métis experience: the open freedom they continually sought as they pushed farther and farther west and the fences that Canadian authorities never stopped building to try to contain a people who were too free, too "Indian" in their outlook. These two places encompass both the promise and the near destruction of a people. They also speak to the two opposing forces that have always made up this country: the wilderness and the desire to constrain it.

During the long voyage of writing this book, I came, early on, to the understanding that in some ways Gabriel represents the "Indian" in the Métis and Louis the European. Gabriel, a master hunter and speaker of indigenous languages, lived on and for the land. Louis, university-educated and deeply Catholic, never seemed fully comfortable in the wilderness and instead continually strove for a way to build his vision of a new church, a new society, in the wilds of the West. And when these two powerful men came together in 1884 and 1885, a truly united Métis world view emerged, one that John A. Macdonald quickly recognized was a threat to his vision of Canada.

These Métis, these half-breeds, our first prime minister realized, could not be controlled on reserves in the same way he tried to control the "Indians." Depending on how one sees it, John A.'s strategy of simply ignoring Métis petitions for so many years either backfired tragically or succeeded brilliantly when Dumont and Riel forced his hand by announcing a provisional government. Ironically or not, John A.'s inaction created the military action that attempted, once and for all, to crush the Métis Nation.

Clearly, though, this nation is resilient. Well over three hundred thousand people in Canada are enrolled Métis, and many, many thousands more self-identify as Métis. The Métis homeland includes regions in nine of our ten provinces as well as the North-West Territories. Métis populations are also found in parts of Montana, North Dakota, and Minnesota. The people, they aren't going anywhere. They—we—are a part of the landscape that is our country.

But do characters like Gabriel Dumont and Louis Riel matter in our contemporary world? Do we need the ghosts of these men in our busy, modern lives? I believe the answer is self-evident, especially when I look across Canada in the twenty-first century. The rebel in me, that person who won't be pushed around by bullies or faceless institutions, sees a direct link between the struggle of a people 125 years ago and the struggles of so many average Canadians today.

As representatives of their community, Louis and Gabriel struggled against the entity that called itself "progress" and took the physical, often bullying form of the surveyor, the politician, and finally the railroad. This, to me, is the same struggle so many of us face today. Modern industry and multinational corporations are our very own contemporary "progress." From our hunger for oil to our over-reliance on personalized technology, we sometimes lose ourselves. I don't argue that progress is a bad thing, just as Gabriel and Louis would not have argued that. But the lesson learned from Riel and Dumont is that progress, in whatever form it takes, should never be allowed to trample the rights of the community or the broader culture. Progress, in all its forms, should serve us, not us it.

That history lesson, for me, is the most important one of all.

SOURCES

When it comes to the life of Louis Riel and, to a much lesser degree, of Gabriel Dumont, the sheer number of primary sources is tremendous. So I focus here on more contemporary explorations of these two men.

Please also note that the following shortlist is by no means complete but just a taste of the brilliant explorations out there. My deep apologies to the authors of the many great books about Riel and Dumont that I've left off the list.

George Woodcock's biography *Gabriel Dumont: The Métis Chief and His Lost World* (Edmonton: Hurtig, 1975) is invaluable and a fantastic read.

Gabriel Dumont: Memoirs (Brandon, MB: Brandon University Press, 2006), edited by Denis Combet, is second to none and simply amazing.

Joseph Kinsey Howard's *Strange Empire* (New York: William Morrow, 1952), considered a mid–twentieth-century gem, is a fount of great research on Riel, Dumont, and the North-West in the second half of the 1800s, but it certainly shows its age at times.

Despite covering only a relatively small part of his extensive journals, *The Diaries of Louis Riel* (Edmonton: Hurtig, 1976), edited by Thomas Flanagan, is a must-read if you want to begin to try to understand the mindset of this man.

The Selected Poetry of Louis Riel (Toronto: Exile, 1993), translated by Paul Savoie and edited by Glen Campbell, is another fantastic way to begin trying to decipher the man's heart.

Maggie Siggins's much debated and studied tome, *Riel: A Life of Revolution* (Toronto: HarperCollins, 1994), is a fine read. Siggins does that thing so many academics fail to do: she brings the man and his world to life.

The False Traitor: Louis Riel in Canadian Culture by Albert Braz (Toronto: University of Toronto Press, 2003) is fascinating.

Prairie Fire: The 1885 North-West Rebellion by Bob Beal (Toronto: McClelland & Stewart, 1999) is a solidly researched and written account.

Chester Brown's *Louis Riel: A Comic Strip Biography* (Montreal: Drawn and Quarterly, 2003) is brilliant and beautiful and moving, a great example of how history can be told in a new and refreshing way.

G.F.G. Stanley's *The Birth of Western Canada: A History of the Riel Rebellions* (Toronto: University of Toronto Press, 1936) and *Louis Riel: Patriot or Rebel?* (Toronto: Ryerson, 1963) remain early cornerstones of serious research and discussion of Riel and the North-West.

Thomas Flanagan's *Louis "David" Riel: Prophet of the New World* (Toronto: University of Toronto Press, 1979) and *Riel and the Rebellion: 1885 Reconsidered* (Saskatoon, SK: Western Producer Prairie Books, 1983) are thoroughly researched and singularly driven.

ACKNOWLEDGMENTS

The writing of this book was one of the tougher creative struggles of my life. It's very easy to feel overwhelmed by the vast quantity of information on Louis Riel and, to a much lesser extent, Gabriel Dumont. Throw into the mix the debate that continues to wage about whether Riel was a prophet or a madman, and it makes for some daunting subject matter. I've learned that writing a historical biography such as this means treading on the sacred ground of a people, and for that, one should always ask permission and seek out the experts in the community.

And so I thank Denis Combet, Métis scholar and gentleman, who read my manuscript with a keen and careful eye. I also wish to thank Sherry Farrell Racette for allowing me to pick her brilliant Métis brain. Another Métis scholar and gentleman, Warren Cariou, gave me incredibly insightful feedback. Thank you for your generosity and time, Warren. To round out my Métis posse, I need also to thank the wonderful poet Kate Vermette for her insightful commentary and Niigonwedon James Sinclair, the man with a plan, not only for his excellent commentary but also for introducing me to so many fine, fine people. Any mistakes or inconsistencies in this book are wholly mine.

And a book like this can't go to press without the great minds of people like John Ralston Saul, who also offered invaluable insight; Diane Turbide at Penguin, who has shepherded this amazing series; and my copy editor, Scott Steedman, who spent countless hours poring over the manuscript.

Finally, *chi meegwetch*, Amanda. I'm a lucky, lucky man.

Louis Riel

1670 English King Charles II grants the Hudson's Bay Company a charter giving it a trading monopoly over "Rupert's Land," defined as all territory whose rivers and streams flow into Hudson Bay. The Company now owns 1.5 million square miles of North America, including more than a third of modern Canada.

1811 Scottish noble Thomas Douglas, 5th Earl of Selkirk, establishes the Red River Colony on land granted to him by the Hudson's Bay Company. It covers most of present-day Manitoba plus a large swath of the northern U.S.A.

1844 Louis Riel is born in the Red River Settlement, near present-day Winnipeg, Manitoba.

1858 Archbishop Taché sends the fourteen-year-old Riel to Montreal to study for the priesthood.

1861–65 American Civil War.

1864–66 Upon the sudden death of his father in 1864, Riel drops out of university and finds work as a law clerk to help support his family.

1866–68 Riel moves to the United States, to Chicago and then Saint Paul, Minnesota, in pursuit of work.

1867   On July 1 Canada becomes a nation. John A. Macdonald becomes the first prime minister.

1868   Riel returns to the Red River Settlement.

1869   In July Canada's minister of public works, William McDougall, orders a survey of the Red River Settlement.

In August Riel gives his first great public address, on the steps of Saint-Boniface Cathedral, warning of the dangers of the government-ordered survey of Métis land.

In September William McDougall is promoted to lieutenant governor of the North-West Territories.

On October 11 Riel, along with Métis supporters, stops surveyors from continuing their work on Métis land.

In mid-October the Métis National Committee is formed.

On November 2 Métis horsemen refuse Lieutenant Governor McDougall entry to their land and he is forced to retreat to the U.S.

On December 1 Riel presents his List of Rights to a convention of representatives of the North-West Territories.

On December 8 the Métis National Committee declares a provisional government.

On December 27 Riel is made president of the provisional government.

1870 On February 17 Riel's horsemen capture and arrest forty-eight men bent on toppling the provisional government, near Upper Fort Garry.

In mid-February one of the forty-eight, Charles Boulton, a militiaman and surveyor, is condemned to death for trying to overthrow the new government. Soon after, Riel pardons him and he is released.

On March 4 Thomas Scott is executed by the provisional government. Riel refuses to intervene. Scott's execution inflames Orangemen in Ontario and will haunt Riel for the rest of his life.

On May 12 the Manitoba Act is passed and Manitoba becomes a province of Canada. Riel is twenty-five.

In June the government of Canada acquires both Rupert's Land and the North-West Territories from the Hudson's Bay Company.

On August 24 the Wolseley Expedition arrives in Red River. Riel, fearing he will be arrested and charged with the murder of Scott, flees to the U.S.

1871–77　Canada concludes seven treaties with all Aboriginal people from Lake of Woods to the Rocky Mountains *(taken directly from Rudy Wiebe's Big Bear)*

1871　　On June 25–26 American Sioux and Northern Cheyenne defeat General Custer at Little Bighorn, Montana.

On July 20 British Columbia joins the Canadian confederation.

1873　　In May the North West Mounted Police (NWMP) are created by Queen Victoria, on advice of Canadian prime minister John A. Macdonald.

In October, while in exile, Riel is elected to Parliament, but he's unable to take his seat for fear of being arrested for murder or, worse, being assassinated.

In November the Pacific Scandal forces John A. Macdonald to resign as prime minister.

1874 In February Riel is re-elected to Parliament, but is expelled before taking his seat.

In September he is re-elected a third time and once again expelled.

In October Riel, along with his friend Ambroise Lépine, is convicted of the murder of Thomas Scott.

1875 In January Riel's death penalty is commuted to two years' imprisonment.

In February he is granted amnesty on the condition that he remain in exile for five years.

1876 In February Riel is spirited illegally back into Canada by friends and family worried about his mental health.

On March 6 Riel is committed to the Hospice of St. Jean de Dieu, an asylum in Montreal, against his will.

On May 19, for fear that he will be discovered by his enemies, Riel is moved to a different asylum, St. Michel-Archange in Beauport, Quebec.

1878 On January 29 Riel is released from the Beauport asylum and whisked back to the U.S.

In October John A. Macdonald is re-elected as prime minister; he will remain in power until his death in 1891.

1879 Riel takes up residence in Montana.

1881 Riel marries Marguerite Monet.

1883 Riel becomes an American citizen.

1884 In late June Gabriel Dumont visits Riel and asks him to return to Canada to once again defend the Métis.

In early July Riel arrives in Batoche, in present-day Saskatchewan, to great excitement.

On July 19 Riel speaks convincingly to a large crowd of settlers and Métis in Prince Albert.

On July 28 Riel's secretary, William Jackson (later Honoré Jaxon), issues a manifesto of the grievances and objectives of both settlers and Métis.

On December 16 Riel sends a petition to the Secretary of State outlining Métis complaints and demands.

1885   In late January John A. Macdonald creates a three-man commission to look into Métis grievances.

In early February Edgar Dewdney, lieutenant governor of the North-West Territories, receives the weak federal response to Métis petitions and, fearing an uprising, passes along a re-imagined version of the telegram.

On March 5 Riel and other prominent Métis, including Gabriel Dumont, hold a secret meeting and sign an oath in which they engage to take up arms if necessary to protect themselves from a "wicked government."

On March 13 the superintendent of the NWMP sends an urgent telegram to Ottawa, warning: "Half-breed rebellion likely to break out at any moment. If half-breeds rise, Indians will join them."

On March 18 Hudson's Bay Company factor Lawrence Clarke tells a group of Métis horsemen that five hundred soldiers are on their way to arrest

Riel and Dumont and that "they ... will answer your petition with bullets."

On March 19 the Métis announce a provisional government, with Riel as president and Dumont as adjutant-general.

On March 26 Métis engage a much larger NWMP force at Duck Lake after the police fire upon them first. By battle's end, twelve policemen and five Métis are dead, with many wounded, Gabriel Dumont among them.

On April 2 Cree warriors from Big Bear's band kill nine settlers at Frog Lake.

On April 24 Métis forces, greatly outnumbered, ambush General Middleton's army at Fish Creek and deal a painful blow to his green army.

On April 30 the priests at Batoche excommunicate Riel from the Catholic Church.

On May 9 General Middleton attacks Métis forces in the Battle of Batoche; his army overruns the town on May 12.

On May 15 Riel surrenders to General Middleton.

On July 6 Riel is officially charged with high treason.

On July 20 his trial in Regina begins but is adjourned to allow time for the defence's preparation.

On July 28 Riel's trial resumes.

On August 1 Riel is found guilty of high treason and ordered hanged, despite the jury's recommendation for clemency.

On September 25 Big Bear is sentenced to three years in prison after being found guilty of treason-felony.

On November 16 Riel is hanged at Regina.

On December 12 he is buried at Saint-Boniface in Winnipeg.

1905 On September 1 Saskatchewan becomes a province of Canada.

1992 On March 10 the Canadian parliament passes a unanimous resolution calling Louis Riel the founder of Manitoba and praising "his contribution in the development of Confederation."

2008 On February 18 Manitoba celebrates first annual Louis Riel Day.

Gabriel Dumont

1837 Dumont is born in Saint-Boniface, Manitoba.

1840 Dumont is taken along on his first buffalo hunt.

1847 Dumont breaks his first horse.

1851 Between July 13 and 15, at the age of fourteen, Dumont is involved in his first military action at Grand Coteau. A Métis buffalo hunting party is attacked by a much larger force of Yankton Sioux, and Dumont helps in the defence, reportedly killing his first men.

1858 Dumont marries Madeleine Wilkie.

1863 Dumont is elected leader of the Saskatchewan Métis buffalo hunt. He is twenty-five.

1868 Batoche becomes a permanent Métis settlement.

1872 Dumont opens a ferry service called "Gabriel's Crossing" near Batoche on the South Saskatchewan River, on the Carlton Trail trade route.

1873 Dumont builds his home there.

Dumont is elected leader of the Saint-Laurent Council, a self-governing institution that sets laws and regulations for the Métis living in Saskatchewan.

1874   Hudson's Bay Company factor Lawrence Clarke
        claims that the Métis, under Dumont's guidance,
        are in open revolt. The NWMP investigates and
        find the accusation false, but forces the Saint-
        Laurent Council to disband regardless.

1877–78 Dumont petitions the federal government for
        Métis representation on the North-West
        Territories Council. The Saint-Laurent Métis also
        petition the government for farming assistance,
        schools, and new land grants. Their petitions are
        ignored.

1880   Dumont leads a successful protest against paying a
        fee on wood cut on Crown land.

1884   On March 22, frustrated by years of silence from
        the federal government, Dumont and a group of
        concerned Métis, along with local white settlers,
        decide to invite Louis Riel to Batoche.

        On May 19 Dumont and a small group head to
        Saint Peter's Mission in Montana to find Riel and
        ask him to come to Saskatchewan.

        On July 5 the party returns to Batoche, along
        with Riel and his family.

1885 On March 5 Dumont, Riel, and others hold their secret meeting to take up arms if necessary.

On March 19 Dumont becomes the adjutant-general of the Métis provisional government.

On March 26 Dumont and his forces defeat a much larger NWMP force at Duck Lake. Dumont is wounded in the head and loses a brother and a cousin in the battle.

On April 24 Dumont and his small force rout General Middleton's much larger army at Fish Creek.

From May 9 to May 12 Dumont leads his men in the Battle of Batoche.

On May 16 Dumont escapes from Batoche and begins his ride to Montana.

On May 27 Dumont crosses into the U.S. and begins his exile.

On November 16 Louis Riel is hanged for treason in Regina.

On November 27 Wandering Spirit and ten of his warriors are hanged near Battleford, Saskatchewan, for their involvement in the Frog Lake Massacre.

1886 In May Dumont's wife, Madeleine, dies.

In June Dumont joins Buffalo Bill's "Wild West" show.

In July the Canadian government offers amnesty to Dumont and the rest of the Métis involved in the Saskatchewan uprising.

In September Dumont finishes his contract with Buffalo Bill.

1887   Dumont gives a number of well-attended lectures in the American northeast.

1888   Dumont returns to Canada, to Montreal, at the request of French Canadian nationalists. He gives speeches, but these go over poorly because of his criticism of the Catholic clergy and their lack of support during the North-West Rebellion.

1891   A lone attacker attempts to murder Dumont while he sleeps in his tent in a hunting camp in the Dakotas.

1893   Dumont returns to Batoche for good.

1902   The federal government finally gives Dumont title to his homestead at Gabriel's Crossing, thirty years after his initial request.

1906 On May 19 Dumont dies of heart failure at a friend's home near Batoche.

1923 Batoche, site of the Métis' last battle and Dumont's grave marker, is declared a National Historic Site.

1980 The Gabriel Dumont Institute of Native Studies and Applied Research opens in Prince Albert, Saskatchewan; it later opens further campuses in Regina and Saskatoon.

COLLECT THEM ALL

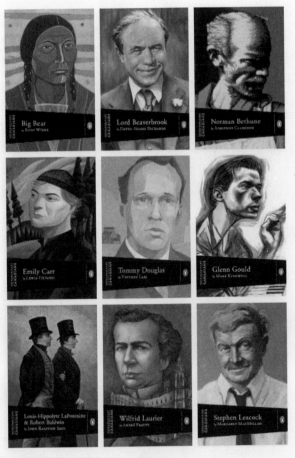

Big Bear
by RUDY WIEBE

Lord Beaverbrook
by DAVID ADAMS RICHARDS

Norman Bethune
by ADRIENNE CLARKSON

Emily Carr
by LEWIS DeSOTO

Tommy Douglas
by VINCENT LAM

Glenn Gould
by MARK KINGWELL

Louis-Hippolyte LaFontaine
& Robert Baldwin
by JOHN RALSTON SAUL

Wilfrid Laurier
by ANDRÉ PRATTE

Stephen Leacock
by MARGARET MacMILLAN

EXTRAORDINARY
CANADIANS

Why They Mattered Then.
Why They Matter Now.

COLLECT THEM ALL